Esse
Athens

by
Mike Gerrard

Mike Gerrard is a freelance writer who has been
visiting Greece for more than 20 years. He
contributes regularly to the travel pages of
newspapers and magazines.

Produced by AA Publishing

Written by Mike Gerrard
Peace and Quiet section
by Paul Sterry
Original photography
by Peter Wilson

Edited, designed and produced
by AA Publishing.
© The Automobile Association
1995.
Maps © The Automobile
Association 1995.

Distributed in the United Kingdom
by AA Publishing, Norfolk House,
Priestley Road, Basingstoke,
Hampshire, RG24 9NY.

A CIP catalogue record for this
book is available from the British
Library.

ISBN 0 7495 0931 7

Published by AA Publishing, a
trading name of Automobile
Association Developments
Limited, whose registered office
is Norfolk House, Priestley Road,
Basingstoke, Hampshire, RG24
9NY.
Registered number 1878835.

Colour separation: BTB Colour
Reproduction Ltd, Whitchurch,
Hampshire

Printed by: Printers Trento, S.R.L.,
Italy

Front cover picture:
Parliament guard

A note on Greek place-names
There are often several alternative versions when Greek place-names are
transcribed into the Roman alphabet. In headings of place descriptions,
and in the Index, this book uses the version corresponding with AA maps,
but more familiar anglicised spellings (given in brackets in the headings)
are sometimes used in the text.

Contents

This book employs a simple rating system to help choose which places to visit:

✓	'top ten'

♦♦♦   do not miss
♦♦   see if you can
♦   worth seeing if you have time

Introduction and Background

INTRODUCTION

Athenian survivor: despite gunfire, decay and pollution, the Parthenon's columns still stand proud

An image of Athens: a scooter rider drives through a No Entry sign, bumps his bike up on to the pavement and heads the wrong way down a one-way street, zig-zagging through the shoppers to get to his destination. It is against all the rules, but it works – and the same applies to Athens.

For most visitors first impressions are not likely to be favourable, and first impressions do tend to linger. In Athens (Athinai in Greek) they will be of dense traffic, smog-filled air, crowded sites and museums, the intense heat of midsummer; of a city in chaos; of constant noise. But who could expect a city of four million Greeks to be calm and quiet? Athens is nothing if not full of contradictions, and despite its incredibly busy nature it is one of the few world capitals that retain a human scale. Where else would you see tiny Byzantine churches in the middle of main roads, the traffic filtering round them? Elsewhere, churches like the tiny Kapnikaria, isolated in the midst of busy Ermou Street, would have long since been bulldozed in the name of progress. And wander down those same busy streets on weekend mornings and you will find stalls and street-traders lining the sides, also resisting the onslaught of traffic. It is a city where, less than a hundred metres from the busy Acropolis, the prepared visitor will find the area known as Anafiotika, a genuine village in the heart of the city where

LOCATOR

*Grecian vase –
20th-century
souvenir style*

tiny whitewashed houses cluster round
cobbled streets so narrow that even a donkey
would find them difficult to pass through. You
could be on one of the Greek islands.

For many, Athens will be a one-night stop-over
en route to or from the islands, through the
city's port, Piraeus (Piraievs), which is one of
the busiest in the Mediterranean. Others will
visit as part of a cruise, or for a weekend break
to take in the highlights. While it is possible on
a brief visit to see the city's two main
attractions – the Acropolis and the
incomparable National Archaeological
Museum – and to dine in the busy and much-
improved old Plaka district, the lucky visitor is
the one who spends longer, and sees more.

A city is about its inhabitants as much as its
monuments, and people-watching in Greece is
always a rewarding activity. The quick visit
seldom allows time to sit in the cafés on
Syntagma, or take a leisurely lunch in a taverna
and watch the world go by. So stay longer and
visit the flea-market of Monastiraki and the
nearby bazaar area, not just the souvenir
shops in the Plaka. Make time to look inside
some of the hundreds of Byzantine churches
dotted about the city, sometimes in the most
surprising places. In addition to the Acropolis,
see the ancient Agora with its wonderfully
restored Stoa, an elegant colonnaded building
that gives a rare chance to see how ancient

You don't have to know Greek to read street signs

Athens looked. Seek out the Temple of Olympian Zeus, the Tower of the Winds, Hadrian's Arch and the Kerameikos Cemetery of ancient Athens. If you can only see one museum then of course it should be the National Archaeological Museum, but what of the Goulandris Museum of Cycladic Art, the Byzantine Museum, the delightful Museum of Greek Musical Instruments, the Theatre Museum or the new Acropolis Study Centre, still taking shape but promising to be one of the city's major attractions?

A longer visit also allows time to appreciate the ordinary everyday life of Athens, such as the raucous meat and fish markets, or the Sunday-morning flea-market which is an assault on the senses and takes place only a few metres from the market of ancient Athens. Some may be offended at seeing pornographic videos on open sale, and yet scenes of equal depravity can be seen in almost every museum in the city, reminding us that although the landscapes of cities change, people remain the same. Did the poor ancient Athenians not also spread a few paltry items on the ground before them to raise a little extra cash, and did itinerant traders not come into the city then and stand on boxes shouting the virtues of their goods, and the cheapness of their prices?

And culture is not merely a dead-and-buried aspect of Athens, as a visit round the city's many modern art galleries will show. Some artists explore traditional themes while others strive for new modes of expression. It is worth remembering, too, that it was a Greek – the much-mourned Minister of Culture Melina Mercouri – who had the idea of nominating a different city each year as European City of Culture. And Miss Mercouri – unconventional, individual – was seen as the embodiment of the modern Athenian, a woman not afraid of driving through a few No Entry signs herself. A city reflects its inhabitants, and that is why Athens is unique, emotional, passionate, warm-hearted, argumentative ... and, yes, noisy, chaotic, and fond of breaking all the rules. The visitor should accept it for what it is, and enjoy it.

One of the great sights of the world: the Acropolis by night

BACKGROUND

Origins

Athens and the Acropolis are inextricably linked in people's minds, so it is no surprise to discover that the earliest signs of habitation were of people living on the southern slopes of the Acropolis in about 3000BC. The settlements were close to what is now the Odeon of Herodes Atticus and the Theatre of Dionysus – the latter still 2,500 years in the future when these first Athenians settled here. Athens can therefore claim to be the oldest city in Europe. The area around the Acropolis became an ideal settling place, with water near by, the rock to retreat to and a clear view down to the harbour at Piraeus. Archaeologists have found remains of houses, wells and graves here, though at this period of the city's history reality and mythology intertwine. The first of the mythical kings of Athens was Kekrops, in about 1580BC. He is said to have had the body of a snake, yet also to have been responsible

AROUND ATHENS

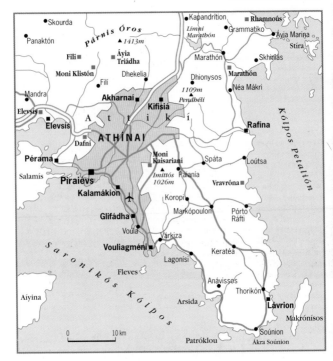

for the first laws of Athens, and for the invention of the alphabet.

It was during the reign of Kekrops that the city of Athens gained its name, which derives from the goddess daughter of Zeus, father of all gods and men; she was known as Athena the Virgin – Athena Parthenos in Greek. The temple known as the Parthenon was later built to house a magnificent 12m-tall gold and ivory statue of Athena. The nearby Erechtheion is said to be built on the place where Athena and Poseidon battled for possession of the Acropolis, Athena touching the ground with her spear to bring forth the first olive tree. Poseidon had earlier produced a spring of salt water, but the gods on Mount Olympus declared Athena to be the winner and rightful owner of the Acropolis.

Myths aside, there is evidence that by 1400BC the area on the top of the rock (Akropolis means 'upper town') had been fortified and turned into a large royal citadel. It was round about this time that the Myceneans arrived, and they were to control Athens until 1125BC: one of the walls still remaining on the Acropolis has been shown to be of Mycenean origin, from 1300BC. The conquerors came from Mycenae in the Peloponnese, at that time a much more important city than Athens. Their most famous ruler was King Agamemnon. A prominent character in Homer's *Iliad*, he was originally believed to have been a mythical king until excavations by the German archaeologist Heinrich Schliemann in the 1870s showed that there had indeed been a flourishing civilisation at Mycenae. The gold burial mask which Schliemann unearthed was, he firmly believed, that of King Agamemnon. He sent a telegram to the King of Greece with the resonant phrase: 'I have gazed upon the face of Agamemnon.' The mask and other Mycenean golden treasures are an essential part of any visit to the National Archaeological Museum.

The Erechtheion, where divinities once battled for possession of the Acropolis

One of the causes of the downfall of the
Myceneans was the Trojan War, the true cause
of which was the Greeks' desire to control
Troy and gain access to all the trade with the
east which passed through this town at the
entrance to the Dardanelles (in present-day
Turkey). Although they won the war, it was at
such a high cost that they never recovered, as
the benefits from it were minimal. Athens,
being a comparatively insignificant outpost,
played little part in the war and so suffered
least from it. When the invading armies of the
Dorians – ancestors of the modern Cretans –
arrived from the north, they took other
Mycenean centres, but Athens was not even
attacked. The citizens were aware of the
threats, however, and those inside the
Acropolis made sure they had access to the
water sources lower down the hill, while those
on the outside of the defences made sure they
in their turn had the right to come inside the
city walls if attacked. It was this negotiation of
rights for the ordinary citizen that led in time to
Athens being the birthplace of modern
democracy. It was not immediate, however, as
the defeat of the Myceneans led to a period

*Early Olympics: a
victor entering the
Temple of Zeus*

Figurine from the Cycladic islands, where civilisation flourished before the rise of the all-conquering Myceneans (Goulandris Museum of Cycladic Art)

from about 1200–700BC during which Greece entered its 'dark age', and that included Athens.

During this time Athens was ruled by kings, and a huge gap grew between the wealthy aristocracy and the ordinary and very poor citizens. It was this period which saw the beginnings of both the Panathenaic – and the more famous Olympic – Games, to amuse the well-to-do. (The 1896 Stadion in Athens is on the site of the original Panathenaic Stadium.) There were no written laws, and the rulers were concerned only with those activities which might annoy the gods. The king was in fact one of three officers chosen from the main families, and his role was to look after religious affairs, as well as preside over the Council of the Elders which met on the rock opposite the Acropolis known, then as now, as the Areopagos (Ários Págos). However, any disagreements between people, as opposed to offences against the gods, had to be resolved by the people concerned. This arrangement naturally suited those with more power and influence, while ordinary people were also helpless to deal with the gangs of armed thugs which were springing up.

Dawn of the Golden Age

Yet from the dark age came the beginnings of the Golden Age of Athens. Demands by the citizens for a written system of law were met, the lawgiver charged with the task being one Draco, whose name lives on, rather unfairly, in the word 'Draconian'. It was thought that many of the punishments listed were excessive – capital punishment for minor thefts, for example – but Draco shared the feeling, and was brave enough to say so. However, his voice carried little power and he was forced to comply with what the rulers had decided. This was around 620BC; a few thousand years on, politics are much the same.

At the start of the 6th century BC, the ruler Solon was responsible for further far-reaching reforms. He drew up a new and much fairer constitution, and abolished some of the harsher punishments, such as unpaid debts leading to slavery. He broadened ruling

BACKGROUND

Detail of an engraving depicting the Athenian victory over the Persians at Marathon

powers by introducing a Council of 400, which met alongside the Council of Elders on the Areopagos. Solon also reorganised agriculture, reformed the currency and encouraged an increase in overseas trade. Under his inspiration, one of his soldiers, Pisistratus, conquered the island of Salamis in 570BC.

Ten years later, though, Pisistratus seized power in Athens too. A native of Vravrona, about 25km east of Athens, he was, for a tyrant,quite benevolent. He introduced yet more reforms, such as a police force (armed with bows and arrows), and set about improving the face of Athens. He began work on the Temple of Olympian Zeus, even though his plans were so grand that work was not finished until about AD130 – 700 years later. When Pisistratus died in 528BC, control passed less successfully to his sons, one of whom was murdered, the other banished when power was seized by Kleisthenes. Kleisthenes divided Attica, the region around Athens, into ten tribes, each of which appointed 50 members to the now-increased Council of 500. It was the beginnings of decentralisation, and of democracy, although not in the modern sense. Each citizen now had a vote, but not everyone qualified for the title 'citizen'.

This was a period when Athens needed to be strong. She defeated the invading Persian armies at the Battle of Marathon in 490BC, but 10 years later the Persians returned and swept through, devastating Athens and the Acropolis, and taking their revenge on a temple on the Acropolis being built to commemorate the Athenian victory at Marathon. The Persian victory was short-lived, however, as they were then defeated on sea at the Battle of Salamis, and the following year finally succumbed to the Athenians on land, at Plataea. But from the devastation of the Acropolis came glory, as the wrecked temple was later to be replaced by the still-standing Parthenon, one of many projects inspired by a statesman whose influence on Athens can still be seen 2,500 years later. The statesman's name was Perikles, and in 443BC at the age of about 50, he became ruler and military leader of Athens.

The face of a philosopher. Knowledge and wisdom were cherished in the time of Perikles

From Perikles to the Turks

One of the Athenian soldiers who fought against the Persians at Marathon and elsewhere was the playwright, Aeschylus. Born at Elevsís, he can be said to be the founder of modern European theatre, as his are the earliest playscripts to have survived. They include the *Oresteia* trilogy, and a play about the Persians. Aristophanes, Sophocles and Euripedes were also all writing in the 5th century BC, and theatre is only one of the arts – and sciences – to have flourished under Perikles. He befriended and encouraged sculptors, writers, architects and philosophers (this was also the age of Socrates and, later, of Plato). But his lasting achievement is visible for all to see today, the glorious Parthenon building which crowns the Acropolis and still manages to dominate the skyline of a busy, modern city.

There had been great changes in Athens during these years, but 431BC saw the start of the Peloponnesian War with Sparta, in which

BACKGROUND

Alexander the Great at the Battle of Issus. Athens was part of his Macedonian Empire for nearly 200 years

Athens was eventually defeated in 404BC. Perikles had died in 429BC. In 338BC Philip II of Macedon added Athens to his list of Greek conquests, his son Alexander the Great going on to extend the Macedonian Empire, which ruled Athens until, in 146BC, the city fell to the invading Romans and Greece became a Roman province. Athens became the city of the Emperor Hadrian, whose Arch can be seen close by the Temple of Olympian Zeus. After the Romans, there followed a long period of Byzantine rule, during which Athens had no important role to play, being merely another small provincial town. With the Fall of Constantinople in 1204, Athens fell first into Frankish and then into Catalan hands, adding to the very varied cultural influences on the city. One of the biggest influences was still to come with the taking of the city by Sultan Mehmet II in 1456, when the Parthenon was turned into a mosque. This began a black period in the city's history, as far as modern residents are concerned, when for nearly 400 years the Turks ruled. It was during this time, in 1687, that the Venetians invaded, destroying the Parthenon in the process.

Modern Greece

In 1821 the Greek War of Independence
began and Athens was taken by Greek
revolutionaries, though the Turks held on to
the Acropolis for another year and regained
the whole city in 1826, remaining until 1833.
Meanwhile in 1830, in London, the three great
world powers of Britain, France and Russia had
recognised Greece to be an independent
sovereign state. They recognised its first king,
Otto of Bavaria, in 1832. King Otto moved into
the Royal Palace in 1833 when the Turks left,
and in 1834 Athens was declared the capital of
the new Greece.

Restoration work began on fallen monuments,
though the city's future was still unsettled and a
long and turbulent period followed. In 1843 a
bloodless military revolution forced King Otto
to accept a new constitution turning Greece
into a constitutional monarchy. Otto himself
was deposed in 1862 and replaced by a
Danish prince, George I. During King
George's reign Athens first saw the glory of
the revival of the modern Olympic Games in
1896, but also the resumption of war against
Turkey the following year.

By 1912 the Greeks and Turks were fighting on
the same side in the Balkan Wars, during
which Greece gained parts of Epirus,
Macedonia and the islands of Samos and
Crete. In 1913 King George was assassinated
and succeeded by King Constantine I, who
was then deposed in 1917 and replaced by
King Alexander I. By now the Greeks had
entered World War I on the side of the Allies,
and helped in the defeat of Germany, though
the Greeks themselves went on in 1919 to
enter Istanbul. By this time King Alexander had
in turn been deposed by the man he had
deposed, King Constantine.

There followed a bloody and ultimately
inglorious few years for Greece, as its army
moved on from Istanbul to capture Smyrna
(Izmir) and attempted to take over much of
Asia Minor from the Turkish troops of Kemal
Ataturk. They reached within 100km of the
Turkish capital, Ankara, but by 1922 were
defeated, the army abandoning Asia Minor and
King Constantine standing down in favour of

*Empires come and
go, but the
everyday lives and
aspirations of
ordinary people
change little
through the ages*

BACKGROUND

In traditional uniform, an efzone guards Parliament, the symbol of modern Greek democracy

King George II. In 1923 there took place an important event in recent Greek history, with the exchange of populations between Greece and Turkey. The influence on Athens was huge, with many of the million or so Greeks who arrived from Turkey settling in the city, and in the port of Piraeus, forced into slum housing conditions. Accounts of some personal histories from this time can be seen in the Tsistarakis Mosque, which houses the Ceramic Collection, some of the Greek refugees from Turkey being talented potters (see page 35). The Greeks brought with them much of the Turkish culture they had absorbed, one effect being on Greek music, especially the *rembétika* songs about the poor living conditions forced on the refugees.

In 1924 King George II was deposed and Greece became a republic, but only for 11 years as in 1935 George was reinstated. The new monarchy was rather short-lived, as the following year saw the formation of a dictatorship after a series of military coups left General Metaxas in charge. By 1940 the Italian army had invaded Albania and was headed towards Greece, only to be resisted by the Greek troops under Metaxas. The general assumed his place in Greek history by a terse response to a demand from Mussolini that Greece should surrender without a struggle. On 28 October, Metaxas gave his one-word reply: *Ohi* (No). Ever since, 28 October has been celebrated as a public holiday, known as Ohi Day. Despite being outnumbered, and with Italy advancing, the Greek troops fought bravely and drove the Italians back. They could not resist the German forces, however, who in 1941 beat back the combined Allied Forces to occupy Greece. Athens itself was occupied from 1941 until October 1944, when the Germans retreated north from the city. This was a period of desperate poverty in Athens, which was not relieved by the liberation as this was only followed by five years of civil war, when Greek fought Greek until the Communist forces were defeated in 1949. The Allies had been pressing the Greeks to restore the monarchy, which duly happened in 1946 when, after the first post-war general

elections and a referendum, the Greek people
restored George II to the throne. The following
year he died, to be succeeded by King Paul,
who was to rule until 1964.

The 1950s saw another influx of people into
Athens, as peasants moved to the city (many
others moved abroad) to escape the awful
rural poverty resultant on what had been, apart
from occasional outbreaks of peace, over a
century of coups and wars, both external and
internal. During this decade unemployment
rose, and in the early 1960s strikes became a
common feature in Athens as people grew
restless with the increasingly right-wing
government, which seemed to be doing little
to alleviate the country's poor conditions. In
February 1964 a new left-wing government
under George Papandreou was elected, but
the longed-for stability did not materialise. The
continuing turmoil, and what was seen as a
slow move back towards Communism, led to a
group of people taking direct action: the
Colonels.

*A citizen of
tomorrow's
Greece*

BACKGROUND

The Rule of the Colonels

In 1964 King Paul had died and was replaced by the young King Constantine II, just 22 years old. He quickly clashed with Prime Minister Papandreou, who was facing allegations that he was trying to advance the career of his son, Andreas (also a government minister), despite claims that Andreas had been involved in a left-wing military conspiracy in Cyprus. Papandreou resigned, but the king refused to order the expected elections, instead trying to form a coalition government. More strikes and demonstrations followed until, on 21 April 1967, a group of colonels led by Colonel Papadopoulos carried out a coup and proceeded to rule Greece with a military junta. King Constantine attempted a counter-coup but was forced into exile when it failed: Greece had proved to be no more stable in the 1960s than it was in the 6th century BC.

The Colonels ruled with severity, despite great opposition both internally and from the rest of the world. Gradually that opposition built up until, in November 1973, students occupied the Polytechnic building at the junction of Patission and Stournara in protest against the military dictatorship. The Colonels sent the tanks in, and an unknown number of students were killed. It was the beginning of the end for the Colonels, however, as in 1974 they took the country to the edge of war with Turkey over the island of Cyprus. The Turks invaded the northern part of the island, the Greek army revolted against their leaders, and in November 1974 the New Democracy party was returned to power in free elections. Soon afterwards, another referendum on the monarchy voted against the return of the exiled King Constantine, and a new republican constitution was drawn up.

By 1981 Greece had progressed sufficiently to be voted in as a new member of the expanding European Community, and in the same year Andreas Papandreou led the socialist party PASOK to victory in the elections. Since then there have been swings right and swings left in the government, and a period of neck-and-neck politics which resulted in several elections in quick succession. The Cyprus problem remains an unresolved legacy of the Colonels' regime, and relations with Turkey are still awkward, though there have been tentative attempts at reconciliation. By 1994 the Greeks had turned their attention to the north, and the attempts of

Athenians delight in political argument, particularly in the kafeneion: *mural by George Savakis*

the former Yugoslav republic of Macedonia (known as 'Skopje' to the Greeks, after its capital) to include 'Macedonia' in its name as an independent state. Greece interpreted this as an implicit claim to the northern Greek region of Macedonia.

Despite their turbulent past, which sounds in the telling like the history of an unstable Central American country rather than that of a member of the European Union and the home of democracy, the Greek people remain among the warmest and most welcoming in the world towards visitors. And the passion that beats in the country's heart – Athens – is what makes it the city of great character which it undoubtedly is today.

What to see

The Essential rating system:

✓	'top ten'

◆◆◆   do not miss
◆◆   see if you can
◆   worth seeing if
     you have time

Orientation

Athens can be disorientating at first, because there are usually at least two of everything. For a start, there are two air terminals, with the west terminal reserved for the national Olympic Airways, the east terminal for all other flights. There are two airport buses, one to take you to Piraeus, the other to either of Athens' two main squares, Syntagma or Omonia – though even this service has two slightly different routes through the city centre. There are two taxi-meter rates, normal and double (for outside city boundaries and journeys between midnight and 5am). At Piraeus there are several harbours, as the unwary visitor may discover all too late when arriving for a ferry only to find out that it departs from somewhere else.

There are two main landmarks in the city, the hill of the Acropolis and the hill of Lykabettos (Likavitós), and it is not unknown for a visitor to reach the top of the latter and

Tranquillity below the Acropolis

ask where the Acropolis is. There are two approaches to the Acropolis, one from the south, well marked and with a smart wide path, the other, on the northern slopes, seemingly designed to confuse visitors who wander through the maze of streets with baffled expressions and bent maps. If lucky you may see a hand-painted sign on a wall, or stuck on a piece of wood, pointing you in the right direction. It is this decidedly low-key approach to one of the world's greatest monuments that gives Athens its unique charm.

The drawback to strolling round Athens is the terrible traffic pollution, and the resulting smog cloud often visible from the heights of the Acropolis or Lykabettos hill. As fast as the government introduces measures to try to control the pollution, so the wily Athenians find ways round them. But just as we are prepared to accept an old friend, with faults as well as virtues, we should accept that this is the way Athens is, and not let it spoil a visit. Instead, find time to relax, as Athenians do, with regular visits to the many coffee-houses, and seek out the lesser-known tourist attractions, which can be a welcome relief from the crowds, the summer heat and the fumes. Don't become one of those tourists who complain about the numbers of tourists: enjoy Athens for what it is.

Information on opening times, etc has been provided for guidance only. We have tried to ensure accuracy, but things do change and we would advise readers to check locally before planning visits to avoid any possible disappointment. Also see **Opening Times** page 117.

ATHENS CITY

◆◆◆
AGORÁ ✓

Reached from either Adhrianou or Theorias streets
(museum tel: 321-0185)
After the Acropolis, the Agora, the ancient market place, is the other major sight that ought not to be missed. Its museum, which contains a small collection of finds from the excavations of the Agora, is housed in what was originally the **Stoa Atallou** (Stoa of Attalos), a two-storey arcade of the 2nd century BC, which has been faithfully and splendidly

reconstructed thanks to the American School of Archaeology in Athens. The resulting elegant colonnaded building gives a rare present-day glimpse of the glory that was Greece. Inside you will find a fascinating and complicated Kleroterion (allotment-machine) from the 3rd or 2nd century BC, used to elect Athenian officials. These were selected at random, acording to how a series of black or white balls fell down a tube. There is also a 6th-century BC child's commode,

Goddess in the Agora Museum

The Agora with the splendidly preserved Temple of Hephaistos

complete with photo of unhappy nappy-wearing Greek toddler demonstrating the device for those who might not know how it was used. Elsewhere is an extract from a set of library rules, dating from the 2nd century AD: 'No book shall be taken out since we have sworn it. It will be open from the first hour until the sixth.'

The rest of the Agora looks a jumble of ruins, though a detailed plan will reveal much of interest, such as the site of the original prison, the ruins of the Library of Pantainos (from which the above fragment came) and the Panathenaic Way. It was along this paved road that the Panathenaic procession wound its way from Kerameikos to the Acropolis every four years to celebrate the Panathenaic Games. The Agora is dominated at one end by the attractive lines of the **Temple of Hephaistos.** Known also as the **Thission** (Temple of Theseus), and lending its name to the nearby Metro station, this

ATHENS CITY PLAN

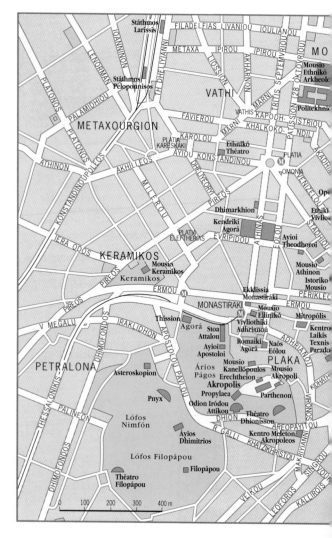

well-preserved Doric temple dates back to the 5th century BC and has, in its time, also been a church and a cemetery.

ATHENS CITY

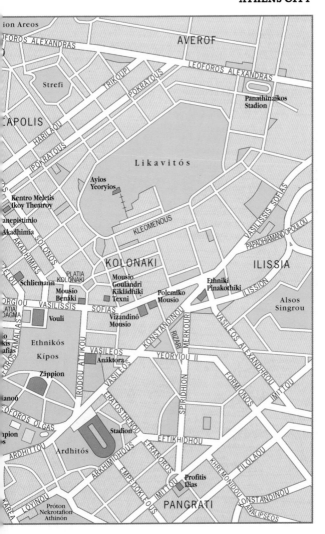

Open: Tuesday to Sunday, 08.30–14.45hrs.

Closed: public holidays.
Metro: Monastiráki or Thission.

◆◆◆
AKROPOLIS (ACROPOLIS) ✓

(Tel: 321-0219)
The prime attraction for most visitors to Athens is the Acropolis. The name means 'upper city' and it was the focal point of Athenian life from the foundation of the city. This huge rock, crowned with temples, is visible from almost everywhere in central Athens, and for visitors driving in from the airport is a stirring sight when it suddenly comes into view, standing timeless and proud above the bustle of the modern-day city buildings. The effect is comparable to a first glimpse of the Pyramids or the Eiffel Tower.

The massive Doric temple called the **Parthenon** – a familiar yet awe-inspiring image – is for most people the symbol of Athens. But the excesses of the 20th century have taken their toll, and Athena the Virgin's beautiful temple is now roped off to prevent further damage from the unending stream of visitors. Acid rain and air pollution have also caused the masonry to deteriorate, compounding the problems brought about by unwitting lack of care during 19th-century restoration work (though these are now being put right). For these reasons, cranes and scaffolding are a common feature of the present-day

ACROPOLIS

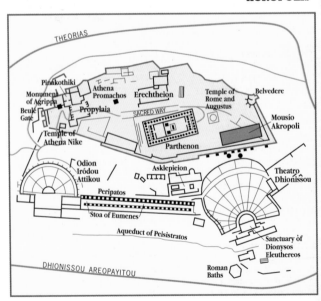

Acropolis – but this is merely the latest of its ever-changing faces.

The Parthenon

The Parthenon and the other main buildings on the Acropolis were part of the 5th-century BC building boom during the golden days of Perikles, when cranes and scaffolding were also well in evidence, as displays in the Acropolis Study Centre show (see page 33). Despite all impressions to the contrary, the Parthenon was built using no straight lines – its columns and beams actually taper gently, giving the huge structure an appearance of lightness. Most of the city's leading sculptors worked on the columns and friezes, though they created a consistently pleasing whole

Prosperity in the 5th century BC led to the glory of the Acropolis

under the supervision of the greatest sculptor of them all, Pheidias. He reserved for himself the right to make the huge gold and ivory statue of the goddess Athena Parthenos which dominated the interior. A model of this statue (destroyed in the 13th century) is on display in the National Archaeological Museum, the best place to gain an impression of how the Parthenon originally looked. Today it looks best at sunset, when iron in the marble creates a golden glow. Sadly for Pheidias, he is believed to have misappropriated some of the gold intended to be used in the statue, and died in prison.

Other Buildings

The Parthenon dominates the Acropolis, but there are other buildings to see. On the left as you enter is the **Propylaia**, the original grand gateway, the holes in its walls indicating where support beams were placed to hold its upper floors. To the right is the small Ionic **Temple of Athena Nike** (Athena, Bringer of Victory). It was demolished by the Turks in 1686, so that they could use its position for military purposes, but the building was thankfully put back together again in the 19th century.

The other main building is the **Erechtheion**, on the left beyond the Propylaia. This is especially important to the Greeks as it is said to be the place where Athena produced the first olive tree (see page 8). The nearby Pandroseion contains an olive tree planted in recent times to commemorate the sacred original.

At the far end the **Mousío Akropoli** (Acropolis Museum; tel: 323-6665) contains an exciting collection of sculpture: statues, masks, pediments and those portions of the Parthenon frieze not taken by Lord Elgin for the British Museum in London (see page 34). Visitors will see that the present museum is too small to house all of the Acropolis finds, and many of these items will slowly be transferred to the Acropolis Study Centre.

Site open: Monday to Friday 08.00–16.45hrs, Saturday, Sunday and holidays 08.30-14.45hrs.
Museum open: Monday 11.00–16.30hrs, Tuesday to Friday 08.00–16.30hrs, Saturday, Sunday and holidays 08.30–14.30hrs.
Bus: 230.
Metro: Thission.

◆
ÁRIOS PÁGOS (AREOPAGOS)

Almost opposite the entrance to the Acropolis are stone steps cut into the rock and leading up to the Areopagos (Hill of Ares), where the supreme court of Athens once stood. The legend is that here Ares, the God of

War (who became Mars to the Romans), was tried by the other gods for murdering one of the sons of Poseidon. It is also where Orestes stood accused of the murder of his mother, Clytemnaestra, and was aided by Athena. And in AD54, St Paul delivered his Sermon to the Athenians from the hill: you can see the text inscribed on a plaque near the steps. The site, which has open access, is of greater interest for its views than the few ancient remains. *Metro:* Monastiraki or Thission.

◆◆◆
ATHINAS/EOLOU STREETS (BAZAAR AREA)
Between Monastiráki and Omonia Squares
Centred on Athinas is the bazaar area, where similar shops cluster together in Middle Eastern fashion and the pavements are lined with stalls. While the visitor may not wish to buy tools and buckets, the food stores are a good source

A tempting array of bottles and nuts in Athens' bazaar area

Athenian Evening *by Iakovos Rizos: a glimpse of Athens in the 19th century (National Gallery)*

of take-home gifts in the form of spices and herbs and offer bread, cheese, fruit, wine and olives for an improvised picnic. A Sunday morning flower market is held near the Platia Ayias Irinis, and there is a large, lively meat and seafood market at the junction of Athinas and Evripidou all day every day. The displays of fresh fish and cuts of meat, and the sheer bustle of the place are a refreshing antidote to a surfeit of history.

◆◆
EBRAIKO MOUSÍO TIS ELLATHOS (JEWISH MUSEUM OF GREECE)
Amalias 36 (tel: 323-1577)
At the junction with Tsangari, look for the number 36 as the museum sign is rather faded, then enter the office building and take the ancient lift or stairs to the 3rd floor. This specialised museum is spread through several rooms,

beginning with the ancient biblical origins of the arrival of Judaism in Greece, through a celebration of Jewish culture and colourful costumes, to the dreadful years of the Holocaust which wiped out completely many Greek Jewish communities, such as those in Kastoria, Crete and Drama. Only larger communities such as in Athens and Thessalonika survived. The museum also contains a 1920s synagogue, moved here in its entirety from Patra, reconstructed and rededicated. A small shop sells postcards and a good selection of books covering Jewish history in Greece.
Open: Sunday to Friday, 09.00–13.00hrs (admission free).
Closed: public holidays.
Bus: 230, 024.

◆
ETHNIKÍ PINAKOTHÍKI (NATIONAL GALLERY)
Leoforos Vasileos Konstandinou 50 (tel: 723-5857/5937)
The gallery is poorly signposted, but look for the ugly modern block opposite the considerably more attractive-looking Hilton Hotel. As a National Gallery it is disappointing compared to equivalents in other European capitals, but worth visiting to see the work of Greek artists, including the best known of them all, El Greco. Breughel, Rembrandt, Goya, Van Dyck and Picasso are among other European masters represented, but even this small collection is sometimes closed while small temporary exhibitions are mounted and dismantled. It was recently closed for several months for refurbishment, with no indication of a reopening date.
Open: Monday and Wednesday 09.00–21.00hrs, Thursday to Saturday 09.00–15.00hrs, Sunday 10.00–14.00hrs.
Closed: public holidays.
Bus: 234.

◆◆
ETHNIKÓS KÍPOS (NATIONAL GARDENS)
The Royal Gardens as they are also known were laid out last century by Queen Amalia, wife of Otto, first king of independent Greece. If you need some respite from the heat and the noisy streets, you will find shade and peace here, with ponds, tree-lined pathways, park benches, cafés and children's play areas. Myriad stray cats and a pathetic zoo are less appealing.
Open: daily, sunrise to sunset.
Bus: 2, 4, 11, 12.

◆
ISTORIKO MOUSÍO (NATIONAL HISTORICAL MUSEUM)
Platia Kolokotronis, Stadiou 13 (tel: 323-7617)
This museum is housed in the 19th-century Old Parliament Building, and you can see the impressive neo-classical debating chamber. The collection itself is perhaps not of great general interest. It includes many busts and paintings, medals, weapons and war mementos. One room has Lord Byron memorabilia; others display folk costumes.
Open: Tuesday to Friday 09.00–13.30hrs, Saturday and Sunday 09.00–12.30hrs (Thursday admission free).
Closed: public holidays.
Bus: 1, 2, 4, 5, 11, 12.

◆
KENTRO ELLINIKIS PARADOSIS (CENTRE FOR HELLENIC TRADITION)
Pandhrossou 36
If you are looking for souvenirs or take-home gifts, try this craft centre in an arcade off the Plaka's main shopping street. You will find traditional Greek art and craft items such as embroidery, paintings and pottery, and also an excellent and popular café/restaurant. Grab a window seat to watch the passing parade below.
Open: Monday to Friday 08.00–18.00hrs, Saturday and Sunday 08.00–15.30hrs.
Metro: Monastiráki.

◆
KENTRO LAIKIS TEXNIS KAI PARADOSIS (CENTRE FOR POPULAR ARTS AND TRADITIONS)
Angelikis Hatzimikali 6 (tel: 324-3987)
A tiny collection of silverware, clothing, icons, silver Bibles and ornate chalices is housed in an old Plaka mansion. It is close to the much bigger and better Museum of Greek Folk Art (see page 39), if you want to see more of this kind of thing, but admission here is free.
Open: Tuesday and Thursday 09.00–21.00hrs, Wednesday, Friday and Saturday 09.00–13.00hrs and 17.00–21.00hrs, Sunday 09.00–13.00hrs.
Closed: public holidays.
Metro: Monastiráki.

◆◆
KENTRO MELETIS IKOY THEATROY (GREEK THEATRE MUSEUM)
Akadhimias 50 (tel: 362-9430)
Tucked away in the basement of the Cultural Centre of Athens, this splendid collection should appeal to anyone with even a passing interest in the theatre. Founded jointly in 1938 by the Greek Playwrights' Society and theatrical historian Yannis

Decorative textile, part of the collection in the Centre for Popular Arts and Traditions

Sideris, these several rooms contain an archive of some 12,000 books and an intriguing collection of theatrical memorabilia. Although the collection is predominantly labelled in Greek only, there are free leaflets available in French and English describing the main items. The star displays are undoubtedly the reproductions of the first-night dressing rooms of about a dozen of Greece's greatest modern actors, and even if the names mean nothing to the non-Greek visitor, the costumes, photographs and personal belongings are still fascinating. Children will probably enjoy these, as well as the puppets, masks and miniature stage sets which are on display looking like so many toy theatres. Another room is devoted to ancient Greek drama, although this may have been rearranged and expanded by the time this guide appears.
Open: Sunday 10.00–13.00hrs, Monday to Friday 09.00–15.00hrs.
Closed: public holidays.
Metro: Omonia.
Bus: 024, 230.

◆◆◆
KENTRO MELETON AKROPOLEOS (ACROPOLIS STUDY CENTRE) ✓

Makriyianni 2–4 (tel: 923-9381)
This ambitious new Athens project, situated opposite the Theatre of Dionysos with its entrance around the side, was already open to the public in 1994, while still under construction. By 1995 far more displays and facilities will be available to the visitor, though the outside is likely to remain a building site for some while yet. Inside you will find an architect's model for the finished site, and if its early promise is realised it will become an essential stopping-off point for visitors to the Acropolis. One of the aims was that the Centre would eventually house the Elgin Marbles, at present in the British Museum (see page 34). It is also intended that other Acropolis remains presently held elsewhere, principally at the National Archaeological Museum, will be brought together and fully displayed in the same place, within sight of their original home.

There is already a great deal of interesting material to see, including fascinating drawings and models showing the full story of the building of the Parthenon, answering the perennial question: 'How did they do it?' This illustrates how the stone was found, quarried and brought to the site, then carved and erected, followed by the building's later destruction and reconstruction in more recent years. There are some original sculptures and friezes on display, and casts of many more, with some of the available space given over to temporary exhibitions. At present most of the information is available only in Greek, but the main information about each room can be read on display boards in Greek and English.

Open: Monday to Friday 09.00–14.00hrs, Saturday and Sunday 10.00–14.00hrs and also on Monday, Wednesday and Friday 18.00–20.00hrs.
Closed: public holidays.
Bus: 230.

One of the Erechtheion caryatids (column statues) greets visitors at the entrance to the Acropolis Study Centre

The Elgin Marbles

The present-day claims by Greece that the so-called Elgin Marbles should be returned from London to their rightful home in Athens has its roots in a complicated history. In the mid-17th century, when the Acropolis was in use by the Turks, who then ruled what we now know as Greece, much destruction was caused on the site by the attempts of the Venetians to topple the Turks. In 1687 the Parthenon, which was being used as a Turkish gunpowder store, exploded causing the loss of the roof and a two-day fire. The ancient stones and statues then lay around on the floor for over a century, some being turned into lime by the Turks using lime-kilns on the site.

This was the situation when the British Lord Elgin in 1801 negotiated with the Ottoman rulers for permission to erect scaffolding, undertake excavations, make copies and drawings of the remains, and take some of them away for study. There is no doubt that were it not for his actions, some of those Acropolis remains would no longer be in existence. The story is complicated by the fact that Elgin exceeded his remit by removing far more than he should, and then selling the items on to the trustees of the British Museum. He received £36,000 for them, but this was less than half what the enterprise had actually cost him. There is no doubt that

Elgin had an eye for an opportunity, but at the same time he was concerned to preserve the ancient monuments.

Another twist to the story is that, after the Greeks won the War of Independence against the Turks, the remains that Elgin left behind suffered in comparison to those which had been removed to the safety and stability of London. Some were cut apart in rather crude attempts to reconstruct the site, while others deteriorated due to the ever-increasing amounts of pollution in the Athens atmosphere. Today the Elgin Marbles are in far better condition than their counterparts in Athens. Despite the fact that Elgin's action – rightly or wrongly – undoubtedly helped preserve part of Greece's historical heritage, there can be few visitors to the Acropolis who do not feel that, morally, the Elgin Marbles now belong where they started life: in Athens.

One of the Elgin Marbles

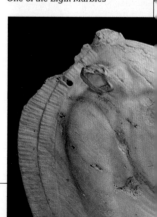

◆◆
KERAMIKI SILOGI APO TO MOUSÍO ELLINIKIS LAOGRAFIAS (CERAMIC COLLECTION OF THE MUSEUM OF GREEK FOLK ART)

Tzami Tsistarakis, Monastiraki, Areos 1 (tel: 324-2066/323-9813)
This enjoyable collection consists of largely bold, naïve pottery, produced by craftsmen who came to Athens in the 1920s as refugees from Asia Minor after the Greek defeat in the war with Turkey (see page 16). Detailed biographical information in Greek and English tells some fascinating life stories.

The pottery is housed, ironically, in a former mosque. The Mosque of Tsistarakis, built in 1759, was used over the years as a jail and a barracks. It suffered badly in an earthquake, but has been sympathetically restored and now provides a bright and spacious setting for the collection.
Open: Wednesday to Monday, 09.00–14.30hrs.
Closed: public holidays.
Metro: Monastiráki.

◆
KERAMIKOS (KERAMEIKOS CEMETERY)

Ermou 148 (tel: 346-3552)
The main cemetery of ancient Athens was in the Kerameikos, the potters' quarter of the city, so called after Keramos, son of Dionysos and Ariadne and patron of potters (hence, 'ceramics'). The cemetery contains tombs and archaeological finds dating back to the 11th century BC (though most are some 500 years younger). Many tombstones have been replaced as they originally stood, lining the grand Street of the Tombs, reserved for the rich citizens of Athens. There is also abundant wildlife here, attracted by the stream that flows rather sluggishly through the grounds. Tiny terrapins can be seen in the grass, in the trees are chaffinches and black redstarts, while olive trees and other plants grow in profusion. It can be a peaceful haven from the traffic of the city, except for Sunday mornings when the noisy flea-market takes place outside the walls. The Museum near the entrance has a good collection of pottery, as well as some very moving gravestones, such as the one containing this message from a grieving father: 'This monument, Xenophantes, your father created for you on your death, Sophilos, for whom you, in parting, created sorrow.'
Open: Tuesday to Sunday, 08.30–15.00hrs, including holidays.
Bus: 025.
Metro: Thission.

◆◆◆
LIKAVITÓS
(LYKABETTOS HILL) ✓

The walk to the top of this 277m Athens landmark will not trouble the reasonably fit, though others may prefer to take the quick and regular funicular service from Ploutarhou (08.00–22.00 hrs). The path winds gradually up through pine-scented woods, and there are plenty of seats to take a breather. Refreshments (predictably expensive) are available at a café part-way up. Another at the top is a popular evening venue for its views across to the floodlit Acropolis. On a clear day the views are uplifting: from the plains and hills around Athens, down to the ships in the harbour at Piraeus. The chapel of Ayios Yiorgios crowns the hill, and below it is a modern open-air theatre.

◆◆
MITROPÓLIS
Platia Mitropoleos
Mitropólis Square contains two very different churches. Completed in 1862, **Megali Mitropólis** (Great Mitropólis) is Athens' cathedral. Its official name is Evangelismos – The Annunciation (depicted above the main doorway) – but it is unofficially known as Ayios Nikolaos, recalling the monastery of St Nicholas that stood here until 1827. The cathedral, more attractive inside than out, is almost

The theatrical entrance to Athens' cathedral, the Great Mitropólis

always open. More appealing is the tiny 12th-century Mikri Mitropólis (Little Mitropólis) alongside, dedicated to Ayios Eleftherios. This church is normally closed, but the exterior is anyway more attractive and interesting than the inside.

Bus: 025.

Metro: Monastiráki.

Bustling Monastiráki

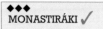

◆◆◆
MONASTIRÁKI ✓

This small square is named after a monastery that once stood here, but is anything but monastic today. As well as a busy metro station, there are cafés and market stalls, and the square is the hub of several areas. To the west is the Monastiráki area, its streets

dedicated to the flea-market, open every day but teeming on Sunday mornings when it stretches along Ermou past the Kerameikos Cemetery – with enough noise to awaken its inhabitants. Stalls sell a bewildering variety of items, from cheap clothes and shoes to expensive cameras, from stuffed storks to *souvlaki*, from religious icons to pornographic videos. Visitors would be advised to watch out for pickpockets, and allow plenty of time for a visit as the street becomes so packed it is often almost impossible to move.
Bus: 025.
Metro: Monastiráki.

MOUSÍO ATHINON (MUSEUM OF THE CITY OF ATHENS)
Paparigopoulou 7 (tel: 324-6164)
This unpretentious small white building on the south side of Platia Klafthomonos was once a royal residence, lived in by King Otto I and Queen Amalia from 1836 to 1842. The refurbished royal apartments on the first floor, furnished as in the royal couple's time, are surprisingly modest, and there are many prints and paintings of Athens over the years. Look out for the detailed scale model of Athens in 1842, when there were only 300 houses.
Open: Monday, Wednesday, Friday, Saturday 09.00–13.30hrs (free admission Wednesday).
Closed: public holidays and July.
Bus: 1, 2, 4, 5, 11, 12.

MOUSÍO BENÁKI (BENÁKI MUSEUM)
Koumbari 1 (tel: 361-1617)
Antoine Emmanuel Benáki was an Alexandrian Greek cotton trader who, over 35 years, accumulated a collection of Greek and Egyptian items which, together with his mansion home, he eventually gave to the state as a museum. The exhibits in this excellent small collection range from Lord Byron's writing desk to Greek folk art (exceptional jewellery) and a painting by El Greco. There is even a complete 17th-century Egyptian reception room. You can round off your visit in the museum's rooftop café or tastefully-stocked shop. Note that in 1994 the museum was closed for refurbishment and features may have changed when it reopens.
Open: Wednesday to Monday 08.30–14.00hrs.
Closed: public holidays.
Bus: 023, 234.

MOUSÍO ELLINIKIS LAOGRAFIAS (MUSEUM OF GREEK FOLK ART)
Kidhathineon 17 (tel: 321-3018)
This museum's only drawback is lack of space. One floor is devoted to silk production, and elsewhere you can see folk costumes, embroidery and jewellery, including intricate silver work. Craft items can be bought in the museum's shop. See page 35 for the ceramics section of the museum.
Open: Tuesday to Sunday, 10.00–14.00hrs.
Closed: public holidays.
Bus: 024, 230.

◆◆◆
MOUSÍO ELLINIKON MOUSIKON ORGANON (MUSEUM OF GREEK MUSICAL INSTRUMENTS) ✓

Dhioyenous 1–3 (tel: 322-9031)
This is a delightful example of a modern, specialised museum in an 1842 Plaka mansion. Each of its three floors concentrates on a different type of instrument taken from musicologist Fivos Anoyanakis' collection of some 1,200 instruments, dating back to the 18th century. You can listen to recorded examples of many of these on headphones, while reading the explanations in Greek or English. The music ranges from the urban blues of

> #### Rembétika
> *Rembétika* is the blues of the Greeks, as distinctive to them as the emotional songs of Édith Piaf are to the French. No one is quite sure how the name or the music derived, though its roots are believed to go back to the start of the 20th century. It developed further in 1923 when over a million dispossessed Asian Greeks returned to their homeland as refugees, settling in slum districts of Athens and Piraeus and adding the mournful sounds of Asian music to the songs of Greece, with embittered lyrics about their poverty and troubles. During the Civil War many resistance songs were added to the *rembétika* repertoire, and these are still performed today in the clubs of Athens (see **Nightlife**, page 99).

rembétika to shepherd's pipes. Look out for the set of photos showing how to make music from the basic Greek combination of worry-beads and wine glass. Videos are constantly showing and there is an extensive collection of Greek music on sale in the shop. Occasional courtyard concerts take place in summer.
Open: Tuesday to Sunday 10.00–14.00hrs, except Wednesday 12.00–18.00hrs.
Closed: public holidays.
Metro: Monastiráki.

♦♦♦
MOUSÍO ETHNIKÓ
ARKHEOLOGIKÓ
(NATIONAL
ARCHAEOLOGICAL
MUSEUM) ✓

Patission 28 (tel: 821-7717)
You will need at least half a
day, or more than one visit, if
you hope to explore fully the
world's largest collection of
Greek art. Among the
highlights are beautiful frescos
excavated on Thira (Santorini),
the volcanic island whose
eruption, around 1500 BC,

*The National Archaeological
Museum, a must for anyone
interested in Greek antiquities*

caused the devastation by
earthquake and tidal wave of
the Minoan cities of Crete.
Perhaps the most popular
exhibits are the treasures from
Mycenae, including the gold
mask identified by Heinrich
Schliemann as 'the face of
Agamemnon'. Familiar statues
include the magnificent
larger-than-life bronze figure
of Poseidon about to throw his
trident and, on a more delicate

Minoan-type vases from the island of Thira (Santorini)

This and the statue of Poseidon were found together in 1927 in the seas off the island of Evia. The stairs to the upper floor are now on your left, but turn right at the foot of these for the prehistory collection which includes the golden masks of Mycenae, and many splendid finds from Tiryns, to the south of Mycenae in the Peloponnese. Note that this display is temporary, but long-running. To the left at the foot of the stairs is a marvellous collection of bronzes including a rampant satyr familiar from risqué Greek postcards, yet so tiny in actuality that many visitors pass by without noticing it. At the top of the stairs, straight ahead up a few more steps, is the collection of delicate frescos from Thira, dating from about 1500BC. Note the two young boys boxing, and wall paintings of monkeys and antelopes. Again this is a temporary exhibition, but is expected to be there for some considerable time. Though reported to be returning to Santorini as long ago as 1990, it was still on display in 1994. If you have longer to spare and would like to know more about the collection, then guides can be hired for personal tours in English, French, German, Italian and Spanish. You can ask for short or long tours, and the booking desk is in the entrance hall next to the stairs which lead down to the basement café, where you will also find a display of casts and reproductions from the

scale, the Little Jockey, the graceful figure of a young boy in the act of urging on his horse.

If time is limited, then the following 'Highlights' tour may help. On going through the entrance doors to the left of the main entrance hall, walk straight ahead as far as you can go, turn right, and a few rooms ahead of you is the statue of Poseidon. At the far end of that gallery, turn right and walk to the marbled central hall where the Little Jockey is displayed.

collection for sale. This is closed on Sundays.

The museum's separate coin collection (entrance on the first floor) displays only a small proportion of its 400,000 coins. It is planned to move it to Schliemann's House (see page 57), and the side entrance to the Numismatic Collection at Tositsa 1 was temporarily closed during 1994 pending this removal. The Epigraphical Collection is also housed in the National Archaeological Museum. This gathers together many of the historical documents found during site excavations, such as inventories, legal decrees and records.

Open: Archaeological Museum, Monday 11.00–17.00hrs, Tuesday to Friday 08.00–17.00hrs, Saturday, Sunday and holidays 08.30–15.00hrs, Gift Shop (tel: 822-1764) open Tuesday to Saturday 08.30–14.30hrs; Epigraphical Museum (tel: 821-7637), Tuesday to Sunday 08.30–15.00hrs.
Metro: Omonia.

The Little Jockey: a famous 2nd-century BC bronze masterpiece

◆◆◆
MOUSÍO GOULANDRI KIKLÁDHIKI TEXNI (GOULANDRIS MUSEUM OF CYCLADIC ART) ✓

Neofytou Douka 4 (tel: 722-8321/3)

This excellent museum was created in 1986 to house the private collection of ship-owner and patron of the arts, Nikolas P Goulandris. The wide-ranging displays of ancient Greek art include fine painted vases, glassware and other items, but the focal exhibits are the beautiful artefacts from the Cycladic civilisation of 3000-2000BC. The statuettes are especially memorable, the stylised yet graceful figures seeming to float within their display cabinets, their shape and texture emphasised by subtle lighting. It will be a rare visitor not tempted to take home a copy from the attractive museum shop. Computers have been introduced to give visitors information about the museum and, in a fascinating but temporary exhibition likely to be moved to the Acropolis Study Centre at some stage, computers also give animated displays of construction techniques used in the Parthenon.

On the corner of Irodotou and Vasilissis Sofias is the entrance to the new wing of the Cycladic Museum, joined to the main building by a glass-covered walkway. This wing is as interesting for the building that houses it as for its contents. It was designed by,

Right: One of the strange, timeless Cycladic figurines in the Goulandris Museum

and was the home of, the German architect Ernst Ziller, the man also responsible for the Olympic Stadium, the Presidential Palace and Heinrich Schliemann's house on Panepistimiou, among other Athenian buildings. Some rooms of the museum display furniture and watercolours, giving an impression of how the mansion looked when Ziller lived there in the late 19th century, with all rooms leading off a circular central reception

Cycladic Culture

The Cycladic islands in the south-central Aegean, though agriculturally poor were rich in resources of copper, marble and obsidian which attracted maritime traders from both Europe and Asia Minor. Trade brought prosperity and new ideas to islands such as Syros, Delos and Naxos, and by the 3rd millennium BC a remarkable and brilliant culture was flourishing there and producing exceptional works of art. Local marble was often used to make elegant figurines which, despite their almost abstract lines, still convey great depth of feeling. They have inspired the work of modern artists from Modigliani to Henry Moore. The statuettes are generally believed to have been connected with the cult of a fertility goddess.

room. Other rooms contain an extension of the main Cycladic collection, with a shop and WCs downstairs, and upstairs space for temporary exhibitions. The most recent is a fascinating display on the finds made at Eleftherna on Crete in December 1990, which confirm the historical accuracy of Homer's account in *The Iliad* of ritual sacrifices. The finds are from the late 8th century BC and include an actual funeral pyre transported from the site, a scale model of the site as scientists believe it to have looked, and a skeleton of a young woman found there with hands and legs bound – probably a human sacrifice.
Open: Monday and Wednesday to Friday 10.00–16.00hrs, Saturday 10.00–15.00hrs (free admission Saturday).
Closed: Tuesday, Sunday and public holidays.
Bus: 234.

Specialist Museums

There are a great number of specialist museums in Athens. The basic details of a few are given here for those who wish to seek them out; note that many operate restricted opening hours.

Ellinikó Mousío Istorikón Endhimátin (Greek Historical Costume Museum), Dhimokritou 7, open Monday, Wednesday and Friday 10.00–13.00hrs only (tel: 362-9513).

Filotelikó Mousío (Philatelic Museum), Fokianou 2, open Monday to Friday 08.00–14.00hrs (tel: 751-9066).

Hadjikiríakio Ghíka Mousío Kinimatográfo (Hadjikyriakos-Ghika Cinema Museum), Kriezotou 3, open daily except Tuesday 10.00–14.00hrs (tel: 362-6266). Shows classic films such as *The Blue Angel, The Battleship Potemkin*, in the private upstairs cinema each Saturday at 18.00hrs.

Mousío Eleftheriou Venizélou (Eleftherios Venizelos Museum), Vasilissis Sofias (behind Venizelos's statue), open 10.00–13.00hrs and 18.00–20.00hrs, closed Sunday evening and Monday (tel: 722-4238).

Silogi Theatrikoú Skhedhiou Panou Aravandinou (Panos Aravandinos Collection of Stage Designs), Municipal Theatre of Piraeus, Ayios Konstandinou 2, Piraeus, open Monday to Wednesday 16.00–20.00hrs, Thursday and Friday 09.00–14.00hrs (tel: 412-2339).

MOUSÍO KANELLÓPOULOS (KANELLÓPOULOS MUSEUM)

Panou/Theorias (tel: 321-2313)
This small collection of religious and ancient art is displayed in a neo-classical Plaka mansion. There are icons from the 14th to the 17th centuries, including some in near-perfect condition, the paintwork still vibrant with colour; jewellery, including a fine gold pendant from the 9th century, and a bracelet from the 11th or 12th century; and some lovely miniature bronzes. Items from the ancient world include Cycladic figurines and Greek pottery.
Open: Tuesday to Sunday 08.30–15.00hrs.
Bus: 025.
Metro: Monastiráki.

ODION IRÓDOU ATTIKOU (ODEON OF HERODES ATTICUS)

Dhionissou Areopayitou
The best view of this restored Roman theatre, built by Herodes Atticus of Marathon in AD161, is from the Acropolis above. It is normally closed, except during the Athens Festival when it provides a splendid setting for drama and music (see page 96).
Bus: 230.

OLYMPION DHIOS (TEMPLE OF OLYMPIAN ZEUS)

Leoforos Olgas (tel: 922-6330)
Though only 15 columns still stand of what was the largest temple in Greece, the site retains its power: a further massive column which crashed

Fabrics and rugs on display outside a Plaka shop give and oriental air to the street

down in 1852 has been left where it fell to give a vivid impression of the temple's vast size. Begun in the 6th century BC, the temple remained unfinished for 700 years until about 130AD, when the Emperor Hadrian finally dedicated it to Olympian Zeus. The ruin is best seen as the early morning sun rises behind the pillars, or floodlit at night.
Open: Tuesday to Sunday 08.30–15.00hrs.
Closed: public holidays.
Bus: 024, 230.

◆
PÍLI ADHRIANOÚ (HADRIAN'S ARCH)

Leoforos Amalias

Alongside the Temple of Olympian Zeus and completed at the same time, this marble arch is believed to have been put up on the site of a 6th-century BC city gate. Hadrian erected it to mark the boundary between the ancient city, on the western (Acropolis) side, and his own new city, in which the temple stood. Accordingly, the inscription on the west side says: 'This is Athens, the ancient city of Theseus', and on the other: 'This is the City of Hadrian and not of Theseus.'

Bus: 024, 230.

◆◆◆
PLÁKA ✓

The Plaka district around the foot of the Acropolis, once a noisy and grubby nightlife area but now smartened and cleaned up, is often denigrated as a tourist trap. Nevertheless this mainly 19th-century quarter is an exciting and lively mix. The main shopping streets are busy Kidhathineon and Adhrianou, but if you walk up towards the Acropolis, into the back streets you will find a village-like atmosphere still exists. Most of the shops sell the usual tourist souvenirs, but there are surprises too. Next door to some vast souvenir emporium you might find a tiny drinks shop, or an unusual specialist such as Stavros Melissinos at Pandhrossou 89, who has made sandals for John Lennon and Jackie Onassis among others. Plaka is a place to visit not once but many times: by day to shop and wander, and by night to eat and enjoy the atmosphere.

A Walk around the Plaka

Athens is not the ideal city for leisurely strolls, but this walk – apart from the beginning and end – keeps the visitor away from the traffic while exploring the heart of the old Plaka district. Without stops it would probably take only about an hour, but it passes several sites and museums and if you call in at some of these it could easily occupy a morning or longer. Places shown in bold type are described more fully in their individual gazetteer entries.

Syntagma Square to the Lysikrates Monument

From **Syntagma Square** (Platia Sindagma) walk south down Amalias, on the right-hand side of the road, until you reach the Byzantine church of Ayios Nikodemos, set back slightly in a paved area. The church dates from the 11th century, but was partly destroyed in 1827 when hit by a Turkish cannon fired from the Acropolis. It fell into ruins but was restored in the mid-19th century and is now Athens' Russian Orthodox church. The bell in the separate belfry was a gift from Tsar Alexander II.

Behind the church and slightly to the left across the street is a pedestrianised passageway which is the top of Kidhathineon, one of the main streets of **the Plaka** district. If nervous about crossing the busy road, walk down to some traffic lights to the right then back up again and turn into Kidhathineon. After about 50 metres you will see a church on your right, and slightly further on your left is the entrance to the **Museum of Greek Folk Art** (*Mousío Ellinikís Laografías*). The church is that of Soteira tou Kottaki and is in frequent use so may well be open. It also dates from about the 11th century but was rebuilt in 1908. Note the fountain in the small garden which was once the water supply for the whole of this part of the Plaka.

Carry on along Kidhathineon, across Asteriou, and the next right is Geronta, a narrow street which leads to the **Centre for Popular Arts and**

Traditions (*Kentro Laïkís Texnis kai Paradosis*), almost facing you at the end of the street. Back on Kidhathineon, continue down past the many tavernas and as you cross Adhrianou the street name changes to Thespidhou. Take the first left, Tripodou, and walk 50 metres to the Monument of Lysikrates (*Lyssikrátous*). Down the street to your left you have a wonderful view of **Hadrian's Arch** (*Píli Adhrianoú*), standing grandly at the bottom. The

PLAKA AND ENVIRONS

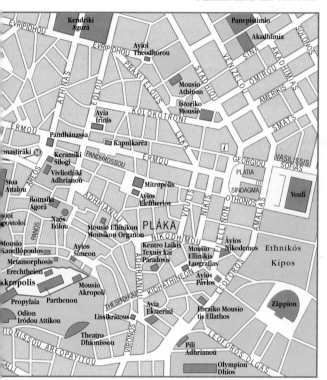

monument in this small square, with pleasant cafés around, has elegant Corinthian columns and celebrates the winning of a tragedy competition by a choir patronised by Lysikrates in 334BC.

Thespidhou to Platia Ayioi Theodhoro

Return to Thespidhou, turn left and notice the studio of George Savakis on your right (see page 50). Walk to the end of Thespidhou, turn right and follow the street around. This takes you well away from most of the crowds which throng the Plaka, towards the Anafiotika district of Athens which clusters beneath the northern slopes of the Acropolis. The name derives from the tiny Cycladic island of Anafi, whose inhabitants settled here in the mid-19th century. It has the fascinating feel of a Greek village tucked away in the middle of Athens. Some of the streets are only wide enough for a donkey to pass by.

George Savakis

In many of the Plaka's tavernas you will see wall murals in a distinctive style – that of local painter, George Savakis. Born in Athens in 1924, Savakis has painted since childhood without any formal training, giving his style a primitive, exuberant quality. He soon established himself as one of Greece's foremost naïve artists. In 1956 he began painting scenes of Athens as he remembered it from his childhood, often on walls both inside and outside tavernas in the Plaka district, where Savakis grew up and where he now has his studio. Sadly some of these have gone, as tavernas have been modernised, but many fine examples remain, for instance at To Ypogeio tis Plakas and I Saita, at Kidhathineon 10 and 21 respectively. Eating places like these tend to be as popular with locals as with tourists and sometimes it can be hard to make out where the murals end and the present-day colourful characters lounging against the wall begin. In the back dining-room at To Ypogeio, all four walls are covered in lively Savakis murals, including a large colourful scene of Monastiráki Square as it was, dominated by the Tzistarakis Mosque, the open square a stage set of characters: the shoeshine man, a boy on a scooter, two old men shaking hands and – an archetypal Greek scene – a man pushing a cart full of chairs.

Savakis's work has been exhibited in America, Paris, London and elsewhere, with some on display in the Greek Folk Art Museum. An 'autobiography' of the artist in images hangs on the wall on your right as you enter his small studio and shop at Thespidhou 14 (tel: 322-6942), where paintings, cards and prints are on sale.

The street you were walking along will bring you to the whitewashed church of Ayios Yiorgos tou Vrachou (St George on the Rocks); bear left here where the main street veers to the right, and at the end, when you seem to be running out of street, turn left up some very narrow steps and immediately right where a hand-painted sign points stray visitors towards the Acropolis and away from someone's garden.

When you meet a steep path at the side of the next church, Ayios Simeon, turn left and walk up for a marvellous vista of Athens and Lykabettos, then back down the steeply-sloping path, looking on your right for the Old University. This was the seat of the First University of the Independent Greek State from 1837 to 1841 and later housed a small historical museum, though this was closed at time of writing. Further on the left note the little Metamórfosis church, inside which is a small chapel dedicated to Ayia Paraskeyvi. The saint is believed to have spent her final few years here and to be buried on the site of the chapel.

About 30 metres beyond this, on your right, is the **Kanellopoulos Museum** (*Mousío Kanellópoulos*). From here you can walk straight ahead and round to the entrance to **the Acropolis**, but if you turn right on to Panos you will see the Museum's entrance. Continuing down Panos brings you to the **Roman Agora** (*Romaikí Agorá*). Turn left to walk round this, the entrance being on the far side, and note, beyond, the impressive Tower of the Winds. The street

Sign welcoming visitors to the studio of George Savakis, chronicler in paint of the Plaka

opposite the Agora's entrance is Eolou, named after the wind god Ailos. The Five Brothers Taverna here can be recommended for a lunch-stop, but if you still have energy walk along Eolou, crossing traffic-filled Ermou, whereupon Eolou becomes a pleasant pedestrianised shopping street, in complete contrast to the very busy traffic-filled Athinas 50 metres away.

Turn right when you reach Evripidhou, which takes you into Platia Ayíoi Theodhorou, where you will find yet another of Athens' attractive 11th-century Byzantine churches. A suitable place to rest at the end of the walk is the very welcoming Café Metro, in this same square.

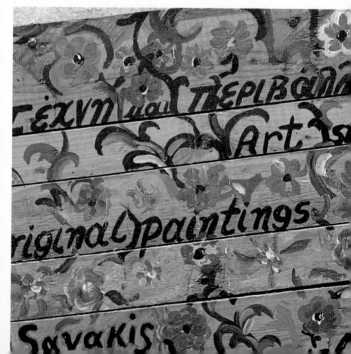

Changing the guard at the Vouli (Parliament), Syntagma Square

◆
PLATIA OMONIA (OMONIA SQUARE)

This is the Square of Concord, but the impression given by this commercial heart of Athens, the meeting place of eight roads, is more one of chaos. Traffic chokes the roadway and crowds throng the pavements and pour in and out of the metro station, shops, coffee houses and hotels. All this adds up to Greek city life at its most uncompromising. In the centre of the square are cafés, a rather pathetic fountain and some half-hearted greenery, but this is undoubtedly the rough side of Athens, especially at night when prostitutes from the nearby red-light district prowl the square. If you need refreshment, there are several old-fashioned coffee houses, full of smoke and arguing Greek males and almost as noisy as outside. A quieter refuge would be the **Bretania** café at the junction of Omonia and Athinas.

◆◆
PLATIA SINDAGMA (SYNTAGMA SQUARE)

Constitution Square could be described as Athens' heart. With its hotels, cafés, kiosks, banks and offices, it is very much geared to the needs of the visitor. Airport connecting services and other buses stop near Syntagma, and most of the main attractions are only a short walk away. At the top of the square is the Greek *Vouli* (Parliament Building), once the Royal Palace. The Changing of the Guards, with the *Evzones* in their colourful uniforms, takes place hourly in front of it (but at 11.00hrs only on Sundays), a ceremony that is one of the Athens 'musts' for visitors.

◆◆◆
PNYX

When the Acropolis crowds have become overbearing, walk down the entrance steps to the south (away from the Plaka direction), cross the main road and look for the sign for the 'Sound and Light Show'. This marks the entrance to a green and hilly retreat known as the Pnyx. Though still busy, its many paths and benches, and the three distinct hills here, mean that some escape from the crowds is usually possible. Most visitors are ferried to the Acropolis in coaches and do not have time, or inclination, to head in the opposite direction. The Pnyx itself is where, in the golden days of Periklean Athens, the Assembly would meet in the 18,000-seat amphitheatre (now filled with seating for *son et lumière*), and

crowds would also gather to hear the great orators of the day.

To the Hill of the Muses

To the left of the main path, as you walk up beyond the entrance signs, a side path leads to the so-called 'Prison of Socrates'. Visitors should not get too excited as these two holes in the wall look more like the entrances to a modern public lavatory and there is no historical evidence whatsoever to suggest that this was the prison where the philosopher Socrates was kept after being arrested for allegedly corrupting Athenian youth with his teachings. He was sentenced to death by drinking hemlock, and actually died in the state prison in the Agora. If you walk past the prison and weave your way upwards you reach the most dramatic aspect of the Pnyx area, the large hill called Lófos Filopápou, popularly known as the Hill of the Muses (147m), on the top of which is the **Filopápou**, the Monument of Philopappus. Though banished to Athens by the Romans, Philopappus was popular with the Athenians because of his generosity and they allowed him to build this grandiose tomb (AD114–16) on one of the city's prime sites. From here there are glorious views over modern Athens, with Piraeus to the south seeming so close you could almost touch it, and with the tiny Dora Stratou Theatre tucked into the rocks beneath you. To the north are views of Likavitós and, of course, the Acropolis.

To the Pnyx

To the right of the main
entrance path to the Pnyx,
almost opposite the Prison of
Socrates, is a Tourist Pavilion
set in the trees, in front of which
is a delightful small church,
Ayios Dhimitrios. It is believed
that a church has been here
since the 9th century, though
the present one was originally
built in 1460 and subsequently
sympathetically rebuilt in 1955.
Its full name, Ayios Dhimitrios
Loumbardhiaris, derives from
the fact that on 26 October
1656, when the congregation
was gathered to celebrate the
feast day of Saint Demetrius,
the commander of the Turkish
garrison then based on the
Acropolis opposite planned to
fire his cannons on the many
Christians assembled in the
church. At the crucial moment
the Acropolis was struck by
lightning, blowing up the
explosives – and the Turkish
commander – and saving the
church on the Pnyx. The church
was then named after the
Turks' largest cannon, the
Bombardier (or
Loumbardhiaris in Greek).
Behind the church and Tourist
Pavilion is the **Pnyx** itself,
though access is limited
because of its use for the *son et
lumière* shows. Further on is
the third hill, Lófos Nimfón (the
Hill of the Nymphs), also
fenced off at the top because it
houses an observatory, which
is open to the public on the last
Friday of each month.
Son at lumière shows on the
Pnyx run from 1 April to 31
October each year. Tickets can
be bought at the pavilion at the

main entrance. There is a daily
show in English at 21.00hrs, in
German at 22.00hrs on Tuesday
and Friday, and in French at
22.10hrs on the other five days
of the week.

◆◆
POLEMIKO MOUSÍO (WAR MUSEUM OF GREECE)
*Leoforos Vasilissis Sofias 22 (tel:
729-0543)*
Spitfires and Tiger Moths on
display outside greet visitors to
the War Museum, built in the
days of the Colonels to glorify
Greek military achievements.
Inside, a large collection on
several spacious floors covers
every aspect of Greek military
history, from the Trojan Wars to
the Battle for Crete during
World War II. It is a good idea
to start at the top and work
down, looking out for the
effective 3-D models of battle
scenes throughout the years.
There is a basement café and
admission is free.
Open: Tuesday to Sunday
09.00–14.00hrs.
Bus: 234.

◆
PRÓTON NEKROTAFION ATHINÓN (FIRST CEMETERY OF ATHENS)
Anapáfsios
Near the Olympic Stadium, at
the end of Anapáfsios Street –
itself lined with businesses
devoted to the funerary arts,
from flowers to photography –
is what is commonly known as
the First Cemetery. This is not
because it is the oldest, but
rather the prime cemetery,
where distinguished citizens
have the right to be buried.
Some tombs reflect the wealth

The sprawl of Athens viewed from the Pnyx

of the families buried in them, but there is room for more ordinary monuments in the cemetery's pleasant few acres: a moving carving of an old man and his wife, her arm resting gently on his, is an affectionate portrait of a long-married couple. Elsewhere you will see too many old photographs of young men in uniform, while the strength of Greek family ties is shown with as many as a dozen relatives buried together in one family tomb.

One of the graves that is of most interest to visitors is that of the archaeologist Heinrich Schliemann, on a small mound beyond the chapel which is to the left as you enter. Schliemann's tomb was designed by his architect friend Ernst Ziller, who also designed Schliemann's House among other distinguished Athens buildings. Schliemann died in Naples in 1890, but his body was brought back for burial to Athens, where he had been living since 1879. Also in the

First Cemetery is the tomb of Theodoros Kolokotronis, the guerrilla leader-hero of the Greek War of Independence. This is on the left of the main avenue, facing you as you enter. Not far from here, but to the right, is the statue known as Kimiméni, the Sleeping Girl, one of the finest works by the sculptor Halepas from Tinos, who designed several other statues in this cemetery, a quiet repository not just of Athens' citizens, but also of the city's life and art. *Open*: daily 08.00–17.00hrs. *Bus*: 4.

Relax with the locals in the National Gardens

The Roman Agora and octagonal Tower of the Winds

◆

ROMAIKI AGORÁ (ROMAN AGORA)

Pelopidha/Eolou (tel: 324-5220)
This is one of the few archaeological sites in Athens scarcely worth the price of admission. Its chief feature is the Tower of the Winds (Naós Eólou), which can in any case easily be seen from outside the walls. This curious octagonal building dates from about 40BC. One of its many features was a water clock, driven by a stream from the Acropolis, while it also has a weather vane, compass and sundials, and a frieze depicting the eight wind gods. One of these, Ailos, gives his name to Eolou Street, at the bottom of which the tower stands. Below here, the mainly ground-level ruins of the Roman market-place are somewhat diminished by an overgrowth of weeds and a pack of dogs which has taken up residence. A small attractive mosque, surrounded by orange trees, is used as a storeroom. Opposite the site entrance are the remains of a *medresse*, an Islamic seminary, which was destroyed by Greeks rebelling against the Turks during the War of Independence.

Open: Tuesday to Sunday, 08.30–14.45hrs.
Closed: public holidays.
Metro: Monastiráki.

◆

SCHLIEMANN'S HOUSE

Venizelou
Almost opposite Zonar's, on the street that is popularly known as Panepistimiou and officially as Venizelou stands the house where the discoverer of Troy and Mycenae, Heinrich Schliemann, once lived. A formerly grand mansion (it was named 'Iliou Mélathron' – 'Palace of Troy'), it was designed and built by Ernst Ziller. Until recently it housed the Supreme Court of Appeal but at the time of writing looks grimy and forlorn. There are plans to transfer the Numismatic Collection from the National Archaeological Museum here after renovation work, but although this was announced as likely to happen some years ago, it does not seem to have been treated with any great urgency (see page 43).
Bus: 23, 25, 230.

ATHENS CITY

◆◆◆
STADION (OLYMPIC STADIUM) ✓

Leoforos Ardhittou
Also known as the Panathenaic
Stadium, this was built in 1896
for the revival of the Olympic
Games. It is yet another of the
attractive late 19th-century
Athenian structures designed by
Ernst Ziller, which tend to be
overshadowed by the
overabundance of classical
sites. The stadium was erected
on the site of the Panathenaic
Stadium, where games were
held from the 4th century BC,
and in the same form as the
ancient structure – the plan
followed the description by the
2nd-century AD geographer
Pausanias. There is little to see,
but its very simplicity is
impressive, especially the
smooth white marble lines of its
47 tiers of seats, which hold up
to 60,000 spectators. The seating
is on three sides only, leaving
the fourth open and looking out
over one of Athens' few wooded
areas, a corner of the National
Gardens. Beyond stands the
inevitable Parthenon, giving the
visitor a feeling of ancient
Athens. The running track is
popular with jogging Athenians,
and the stadium's geometric
lines with photographers.
.Access is free. The Stadion is
not to be confused with the
modern Olympic Stadium, built
in 1982 on a 100-hectare site
near the Irini metro station in the
northern suburbs.
Open: Daily, dawn till dusk.
Bus: 2, 4, 11, 12.

The 19th-century marble Stadion

Ruins of the great library built under the rule of Hadrian

times, when wild animals were set to fight each other in the arena.
Open: daily, 08.30–14.30hrs.
Bus: 230.

◆

VIVLIOTHÍKI ADHRIANOÚ (LIBRARY OF HADRIAN)
Eolou
Close to the Roman Agora is the library complex built by the Emperor Hadrian some time after AD132. As well as the library building, there was a courtyard containing 100 columns (long vanished) and a central pool. The site has been closed to the public for some time while excavations are undertaken, but when it is eventually reopened visitors will be able to see the library which had recesses for storing rolled manuscripts.
Metro: Monastiráki.

◆◆

VIZANDINÓ MOUSÍO (BYZANTINE MUSEUM)
Leoforos Vasilissis Sofias 22 (tel: 723-1570)
This splendid specialist collection is housed in a lovely mid-19th-century aristocratic villa. The collection consists largely of icons, many in glorious glowing colours, but there are also liturgical vessels and vestments, bibles and mosaics. In the far building is a reconstructed early Christian basilica and a complete recreated Byzantine church.
Open: Tuesday to Sunday 08.30–15.00hrs.
Bus: 234.

◆

THÉATRO DHIONISSOU (THEATRE OF DIONYSUS)
Leoforos Dhionissou Areopayitou (tel: 322-4625)
On the southern slopes of the Acropolis, this theatre – much reconstructed and altered over the ages – held 17,000 people in 64 tiers when it was the site for an annual drama festival. Here the citizens of Athens would witness the premiers of plays by the great dramatists of the Golden Age of Athens (see page 13). Look out for the crouching Dionysian figures supporting the stage, and the marble barriers from Roman

PIRAEUS

Piraeus (Piraiévs in Greek) is easily accessible from central Athens, being at the end of the Metro line, though its charms are limited: imagine the traffic of Athens, add the bustle of one of the Mediterranean's busiest ports, and remove the compensations of museums and classical sites. Nevertheless, it can be worth a trip out on a Sunday morning when the **flea-market** operates in the streets behind the Metro/railway station. This rivals the simultaneous market along Ermou in Athens, but is more of a spectacle for the average visitor than a likely place to find souvenirs. However, it is a part of the street life that harks back to the award-winning 1959 film, *Never on a Sunday*, which starred Melina Mercouri as a Piraeus prostitute with the proverbial heart of gold.

If you turn left out of the station and follow the harbour-front round, you will come in a few minutes to the quieter retreat of the magnificent Cathedral of **Ayia Triadha (Holy Trinity)**, with its huge dome and its gallery, the walls a mass of frescos and icons. Destroyed in 1944, it was rebuilt 1958–62 in its original Byzantine style. It provides a wonderful haven of peace in Piraeus.

Museums

It was on Filonos, behind the Town Hall which is opposite the Cathedral, that workmen in 1959 found the impressive bronze statues which form the principal reason for visiting Piraeus's **Archaeological Museum** in Harilaou Trikoupi (near the junction with Alkiviadou). The exhibits in the first hall were found in 1930–1 in a ship that had been bound for Italy and which was discovered in Piraeus harbour. Given the immense weight of stone in it, it seems unsurprising that it sank. All the statues, frescos and carvings were from the same Attic workshop and date from roughly the 2nd century AD. Elsewhere there is the huge head and shoulders of a larger-than-life statue of the Emperor Hadrian, while upstairs are the bronze statues mentioned above, about 2.5–3m high and dating from the 4th century BC. They include Apollo and Artemis, and are displayed to great effect, the lighting emphasising their imposing nature. Also here is a bronze mask of similar date – a frightening, grimacing face – once used by tragic actors.

Turn left out of the Museum entrance and walk straight down the main street to the Limin Zeas harbour. Turn right here and a short way along the front across the street is the modern building which houses Piraeus's other museum, the **Naval Museum of Greece**. This includes model ships, from ancient triremes to modern-day battleships, with displays covering some of the great naval battles in Greek waters, such as the Battle of Salamis, along with documents and drawings, letters and relics. The museum building itself includes part of the **Akti Themistokleous**, the ancient city walls completed in the 5th century BC to defend the harbour and town of Piraeus.

Harbours

For visitors leaving Athens via Piraeus, it is important to know that there are several harbours within the Grand Harbour itself, and because the various entrances to these can be some distance apart it is vital that you establish which harbour your boat will be leaving from. To complicate matters, 'Flying Dolphins' (hydrofoils) for the Argo-Saronic islands and some ports on the Greek mainland leave from the Zea Marina (where the Naval Museum is). There is yet another harbour, the **Mikrolimano**, though this is now known mainly as being the place where Athenians go to find the best fish tavernas, for a leisurely summer Sunday lunch or evening meal. There is little to choose between **Zorba's**, **Mykonos** or **Psrapoulou**, all on the harbourfront, and all safely

recommended. The best food in Piraeus, however, is at the old-established **Vassilenas**, at Etolikou 72 (tel: 461-2457), not far from the Metro station following the main harbour around to the right. In its 70 years it has served everyone from ordinary Athenians to Aristotle Onassis, Tyrone Power and Sir Winston Churchill. Despite that, it is not overly expensive and its traditional menu, comprising at least 16 courses, guarantees a unique Athenian eating experience.

Arkheologikó Mousío Pireá (Piraeus Archaeological Museum), Harilaou Trikoupi 31 (tel: 452-1598), open Tuesday to Sunday 08.30–15.00hrs. **Nautikó Mousío Elládhos** (Naval Museum of Greece), Akti Themistokleous (tel: 451-6822), open Tuesday to Saturday 08.30–13.30hrs.

Piraeus is first stop for the islands

EXCURSIONS

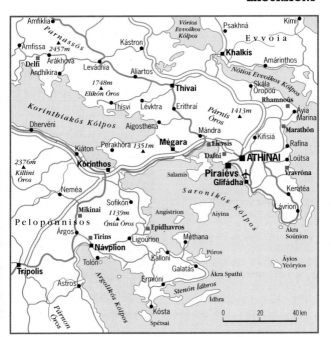

EXCURSIONS FROM ATHENS

There is such a wide variety of excursions available from Athens that it would be hard for the visitor with limited time to choose between them. Some splendid classical sites such as Cape Sounion can be visited in a morning by public transport, and even the magnificent Delfí – regarded in ancient Greece as the centre of the universe – can be seen on a day trip by coach. On the western edge of the city is the monastery of Dafní, a popular spot in summer for its wine festival, while the Kaisariani monastery is a shorter distance to the east, yet is much more remote and peaceful. Stirring names like Marathon and the Elysian Fields beckon, although not all live up to the promise of their name, yet it is hard to resist the temptation to see them for yourself.

It is also difficult to resist the pull of the Greek islands, with Piraeus even offering visitors the chance to spend a few days on far-distant Crete before returning: there are two daily ferries making the 12-hour trip. Closer to the city are the main Argo-Saronic islands of Salamis, Aíyina (Aegina),

EXCURSIONS FROM ATHENS

Spétsai, Póros and Ídhra
(Hydra). These are well served
by regular quick hydrofoils
from Piraeus, and it is quite
feasible to be in Omonia
Square at 07.00hrs, and eating
breakfast on Aegina by
09.00hrs: the metro takes 30
minutes, and the hydrofoil a
further 40.

The visitor will need to choose,
by inclination, time and
finances, which places to visit,
how to get there and how long
to stay. Most are reachable by
public transport, and even if
the return journey proves
problematical, overnight stays
outside Athens are not
expensive. It would probably
be cheaper to arrange things
yourself and pay for a night in a
hotel than to join one of the
organised day trips. If,
however, you prefer to have
the comfort of a coach, and to
have all the arrangements
made for you, then most hotels
and travel agents can offer a
good choice of trips. There are
day trips to Delfi and the
islands, or visits of 3–4 days or
more. You will see trips of a
few days on offer to popular
Cycladic islands such as
Mykonos and Santorini (Thira).
If booking through a travel
agent, though, try to use one
that has been recommended to
you. The vast majority are
honest and reputable, but
there have been a few
incidents reported in the
Greek press recently of 'hole-
in-the-wall' operators setting
up shop, taking 'bookings', and
disappearing. There is no need
to be over-cautious – simply
sensible.

◆◆
ÁKRA SOÚNION (CAPE SOUNION)
65km southeast of Athens
(tel: 0292-39363)
Drive to Cape Sounion, the
headland at the end of the Attica
peninsula, along the Athens
coastal road to experience a
breathtaking first glimpse of the
magnificent white ruins of the
Temple of Poseidon, standing
proud at the highest point. The
marble temple, of which 15
columns remain, is dated to
444BC. The English poet and
Graecophile, Lord Byron,
scratched his name on a
column, but others can no
longer emulate him as the

Temple is now roped off to help preserve it from the loving attentions of its swarms of visitors – many of whom come to enjoy one of the dramatic sunsets for which the cape is famed..

Open: Monday to Saturday 09.00hrs–sunset, Sunday 10.00hrs–sunset.
Bus: buses marked 'Σουvio' leave the terminal at 260 Odhos Liossion, Athens, hourly between 06.30 and 18.30hrs, returning 06.30–20.00hrs. The journey time is 90 minutes. There are also buses on the hour, but these go by the inland rather than the more pleasant coastal road.

The glorious ruined Temple of Poseidon on Cape Sounion

◆
DAFNÍ (DAPHNI)
10km west of central Athens (tel: 581-1558)
Only a short distance from the multi-lane Athens–Corinth highway, the 11th-century monastery at Dafní contains some of the finest Byzantine mosaics in the country. Glistening with gold, the awe-inspiring Christ Pantocrator (Ruler of All) fills the dome, and immediately below are the Annunciation, Nativity, Baptism and Transfiguration. This pleasant but not particularly

Dome mosaic, Dafní monastery

special place has little else to
offer the visitor, much of the
rest of the tiny monastery being
closed. The name Dafní goes
back to the sanctuary of Apollo
that once stood here (the
laurel, or daphne, was sacred
to the god), and there is
perhaps a hint of its pagan
origins when it is the scene for
a festival of wine-tasting,
accompanied by food, music
and dancing, that takes place
here in July to September.
Open: Usually Tuesday to
Sunday, 08.30–17.00hrs, but
variable.
Closed: public holidays.
Bus: 873 from Odhos
Dheliyioryi, every 30 minutes
from 06.00–21.00hrs.

◆◆◆
DELFÍ (DELPHI)
*60km northwest of Athens (tel:
0265-82313)*
A full and rewarding day-trip
from Athens is to the sacred site
of Delfi, in the shadow of Mount
Parnassós. For almost 2,000
years pilgrims came here, to
consult the oracle and to
worship in the temples, whose
fine remains still weave a magic
spell. There is a great deal to
see: the mountains and villages,
the olive-filled valley tumbling
down to the sea, the museum
and of course the ruins –
temples, the Sacred Way, the
Rock of the Sibyl, theatre,
stadium and much else
besides.
Open: site Monday to Friday
07.30–17.15hrs, Saturday,

Sunday and public holidays
08.30–14.45hrs; museum
Monday 11.00–17.15hrs, other
days as above.
Bus: five daily from Athens. The
site is a short walk from Delfí
village.

◆
ELEVSÍS (ELEUSIS)
*20km west of central Athens (tel:
554-6019)*
One of the most sacred sites of
the ancient world is now almost
lost in a wasteland of petrol
refineries and other industrial
installations. Elevsís was the
home of the Eleusinian
Mysteries, with rites so secret
that scholars can only
speculate about them.
Whatever rituals they went
through, in homage to the
goddess Demeter, it is
believed the initiates were
promised resurrection and
eternal life. By the 5th century
BC, the cult had up to 30,000
followers who took part in an
annual procession from Athens
along the Sacred Way to
Elevsís. Imagination is required
to reawaken some of the
ancient magic that the site,
despite the grimness of its
present-day setting, still
retains. Foundations, pathways
and fallen stones are all that
remain, although the museum
has two interesting
reconstructions of the
Sanctuary of Demeter, which
restores a little of the sense of
history.
Open: Tuesday to Sunday
08.30–15.00hrs.
Closed: public holidays.
Bus: 853 or 862; regular
service from Platía Eleftherías.

◆◆
KAISARIANÍ
*7km east of Athens (tel: 723-
6619)*
The church of this monastery at
the eastern extreme of the city
of Athens was built in roughly
the year 1000. The name
derives from the imperial
(*kaisariane*) spring which still
flows from the courtyard and
which the Emperor Hadrian
used as the source of Athens'
water supply, conveying it to
the city by building an
aqueduct. The water, and the
altitude (450m), make this a
cool retreat in the summer.
There are other monastic
buildings, frescos, gardens and
pinewoods to be seen, making
it well worth the trip out. The
village of Kaisariani is most
easily reached by taxi.
Open: Tuesday to Sunday,
08.30–15.00hrs.
Closed: public holidays:

◆◆
KIFISIÁ
15km north of Athens
This suburb at the northern end
of the metro line has long been
an enviable address in Athens.
At 276m its cooler climate
attracts the wealthier citizens,
as a glance at the high street
shops will indicate. It is an
attractive and easy day out for
the visitor too, though not all
north-bound trains go all the
way to Kifisiá, so check the
destination board first. Those
that do, pass the modern
Olympic stadium at Irini. From
the Kifisiá stop walk up through
the park, cross the busy road
and continue up, perhaps
pausing on the left at **Varsos,**

said to be the oldest of Athens' many *zaharoplasteions* (patisseries) . A left turn at the next junction takes you to the **Goulandris Natural History Museum**, a small but impressive collection which naturally concentrates on the flora and fauna of Greece. It is especially good on birds, butterflies and sea shells, and on problems of the environment.

Mousío Fisikís Istorías Goulandrí (Goulandris Natural History Museum), Levidou 13 (tel: 808-6405), open Saturday to Thursday, 09.00–14.00hrs.

◆ MARATHÓN

41km northeast of Athens (tel: 0294-55155)
The site of Marathon does not live up to the fame of its name; see it if you are in the area, but it scarcely merits a special trip from Athens. In 490BC, at the Battle of Marathon, the Greeks defeated the Persians. According to the story, a Greek soldier in full battle armour ran the 41km to Athens with news of the victory, only to drop dead after making his announcement. This heroic tale is commemorated in the modern marathon race, covering the same distance as did the athletic warrior. The 192 Athenian soldiers who died in the battle (as against a reported 6,400 Persians) were buried under a 12m-high mound, still to be seen. The small museum a few minutes' drive away contains interesting items, including carved gravestones, a 5th-century BC

boundary stone, and the skeleton of a child who was buried in a beehive. Walk up the track beside the museum for a panoramic view of the fertile Plain of Marathon.
Open: museum Tuesday to Sunday, 08.30–15.00hrs.
Closed: public holidays.
Bus: hourly from Odhos Mavromateon (orange bus marked 'Μαραθωνασ').

◆◆ RHAMNOÚS

50km northeast of Athens (tel: 0294-63477)
Isolated at the end of a rough and bumpy track, this remote site amid groves of vine and olive has few human visitors.

You are likely to share the solitude only with the birds and butterflies which abound here. The area was sacred to two goddesses, but little remains of their temples – only the base of that dedicated to Themis (built around 500BC), its columns no more than a metre or two in height, and the remains of the slightly later, larger but never completed Temple of Nemesis. If you make the effort to come here, you will enjoy a sense of discovering the place for yourself – something rare in Greece today.

Open: Monday to Saturday, 07.00–18.00hrs, Sunday 08.00–18.00

Closed: public holidays.

◆◆◆
SARONIKÓS KÓLPOS (SARONIC GULF)

The islands of the Saronic Gulf make for a wonderful escape from Athens – as the Athenians know all too well, which is why many of them own houses on the islands. At weekends or at the height of summer, visitors might be better advised to opt for an organised trip with guaranteed places, rather than run the risk of not being able to get a ticket for the overcrowded ferries. Once there, though, there is plenty of opportunity for relaxation, for lying on beaches and strolling

Tomb mound at Marathon

EXCURSIONS FROM ATHENS

down small-town streets not jammed with traffic. If the streets are packed with other visitors, a short walk out of each island's main town will quickly take you to the rural Greece of small villages, or farming and fishing communities, and an unhurried pace of life.

The nearest island, **Salamis**, is too close to Athens' industrial shores to offer safe swimming, but even here you have the opportunity to walk on country

The ferry from Piraeus approaching the island of Póros

roads rather than city streets, to see villages and pine forests – and all a few minutes and a few drachmas by ferry from Piraeus.

Much more attractive – and more popular and expensive – is **Aíyina**. The main town has a busy harbour, with shops and restaurants that cater to the many visiting Athenians, but there are some appealing neo-classical buildings hidden away, and the island does have historical importance. Its early coinage became standard throughout the Greek world, the islanders invented a

standard system of weights and measures, and more recently it was of great strategic importance in the War of Independence against the Turks. Visitors should not miss the superb Sanctuary of Aphaia, about 12km from the main town. The 5th-century BC temple is in ruins, but it has retained its atmosphere and offers a splendid view back to the city of Athens.

Póros is the next island, and while it is scarcely less crowded than Aíyina, it does start to give more of a feel of typical Greek island life – of tourism and tavernas, of fishing and ferries. It is also only 400m from the Pelopennesian mainland, and a quick trip across on one of the small boats that sail back and forth offers an escape from crowds. A short walk away from the mainland village of Galatás is the delightful Limonodhassos, where thousands of lemon trees scent the air and a small taverna offers a taste of fresh lemonade.

Ídhra is a rocky island, but chic and expensive, the St Tropez of the Saronic Gulf. It is undeniably attractive, its one main town with many 19th-century houses clustered round a harbour, and a total ban on traffic – except for the island's dustcart. It has a wealthy past, and a reputation as an artistic retreat in the present: a pleasant place to spend a day or more, wandering round and relaxing.

Spétsai is the furthest distant of these islands, in fact tucked around the corner in the Argolic Gulf (Argolikós Kólpos). Distance doesn't mean an escape from the crowds, but it is a greener island than most, with opportunities for walking. This island is renowned as the setting for the novel and film, *The Magus*, whose author John Fowles taught at the Anargyrios School, near the Spetses Hotel.

◆
VRAVRÓNA (BRAURON)
Near the village of Vravrona, 25km east of Athens (tel: 0294-71020)
The site and museum of Brauron are both on the edge of the modern village of the same name. Pleasantly situated at the foot of a hill a little inland from the marshy coast, the site was occupied from pre-Mycenean times and became an important centre for the cult of Artemis, goddess of fertility as well as patron of unmarried girls and chastity. There are remains of a 5th-century BC temple to the goddess, built over an earlier building. Also here is the tiny late-Byzantine chapel of Ayios Yioryios, and the still-flowing sacred spring. Finds from the site are displayed in a pleasant modern museum 15 minutes' walk away: statues in an open courtyard, pottery and a reconstructed model of the Temple of Artemis inside.
Open: Tuesday to Sunday, 08.30–15.00hrs; Museum, Monday 12.30–19.00 hrs, Tuesday to Friday 08.00–19.00 hrs, Saturday, Sunday and public holidays 08.30–15.00hrs. *Site closed*: public holidays. *Bus*: 304 from Athens to Artemi, then a 2km walk.

Peace and Quiet

*Wildlife and Countryside
in and around Athens
by Paul Sterry*

Introduction

Athens has been a centre of population and culture for thousands of years and the temples, ruins – and indeed all aspects of the city's history – are important lures for visitors. However, Athens, its environs and adjacent areas of mainland Greece offer an alternative historical perspective for visitors – its natural history is as rich and diverse as its human history.

On arriving in Athens, visitors could be forgiven for assuming that a city beset with pollution from car exhaust fumes is hardly the best place to look for wildlife. Yet a surprising variety of plants and animals live alongside man, often colonising the very ruins and monuments most popular with visitors. Travel even a short distance from the city and you can find everything from stunning coastal scenery to classic, herb-rich Mediterranean habitats and towering mountain peaks.

Quiet charm in a backstreet on the island of Ídhra, popular with tourists and artists

City and Surroundings

Visitors to Athens with a natural history interest will find the greatest variety of wildlife during spring and early summer, that is from late February to June. In keeping with the Mediterranean region as a whole, many of the region's plants grow during the mild and damp winter months, flower in the early spring and wither by the summer. Many of the birds of the Greek mainland are migrants, arriving in spring and departing by late summer.

From April to July, the skies over Athens ring to the sound of screaming swifts, as aerial parties of these scythe-winged birds pursue each other through the air catching insects on the wing in their capacious mouths. Also seemingly everywhere are serins, tiny yellow birds whose jingling songs enliven even the smallest parks and gardens. At the start of the breeding season and during spring migration from late March to May, a range of other songbirds can be found in leafy gardens within the city. Try visiting the Acropolis slopes, Syntagma Square and

PEACE AND QUIET

Wildlife flourishes on Likavitós

the National Gardens, but remember that early mornings are best.
For the greatest variety of wildlife within the city boundaries, visit the slopes of Likavitós, the highest of the hills that dominate Athens. In spring, the wooded and scrub-covered slopes harbour such notable songsters as nightingales and golden orioles as well as less distinctive warblers and shrikes. Even the ruins in and around the city can be good for wildlife. Lizards and grasshoppers clamber over the rocky surfaces and birds such as rock nuthatches and blue rock thrushes have

Wildlife and the seasons

The Mediterranean climate experienced by Athens and other coastal regions of Greece has a profound influence on the wildlife. The climate is one of extremes with hot, dry summers and relatively mild, wet winters. Plant growth mostly starts with the first autumn rains and continues through the winter until spring when flowers are produced and set seed. By summer, many plants have withered and died back. Many animals such as insects and snails remain dormant during the hot summer, with most activity occurring in winter and spring.

even been seen on the Acropolis.

Further afield, visitors may like to visit Mount Parnes (Párnis Óros) which lies roughly 30km to the north of the city and is accessible from Ayia Trias. The hills and mountain are carved in places by gorges and the slopes covered with forests of oaks, plane trees, firs and pines and coniferous forests. Beneath the trees is an understorey of kermes oaks and strawberry trees along with colourful flowers and butterflies and birds. A network of roads allows exploration.

Here, and at Imittós (Hymettos) to the south of Athens, birds of prey and storks can sometimes be seen flying overhead on migration from March to May and again from August to October. This latter site is rather denuded of tree cover and instead is cloaked in the dense and aromatic shrub vegetation so typical of many parts of the Mediterranean: flowers and leaves of sages, lavenders and brooms combine to create a heady fragrance which complements the colourful spring flowers of cistuses, orchids and irises.

Delfí
Mountain birds in a stunning, rugged setting.
This popular excursion destination is not only one of Greece's most stunningly attractive historic sites, but is arguably the easiest and best place to observe its mountain birds. Against a backdrop of the mountains of Parnassós, if you scan the skies you will see

---

Ferry crossings
Boat trips and ferry crossings can be rewarding and relaxing ways to observe wildlife. Yellow-legged gulls occur in small numbers around harbours and ports, their numbers augmented in the winter months by other gull species from northern Europe. Watch for Cory's shearwaters flying with stiff wings, low over the water, sometimes accompanied by smaller Yelkouan shearwaters. Lucky and keen-eyed travellers may even see a loggerhead turtle in the water, especially from boats to and from the islands of Zákinthos and Kefallinía (Cephalonia), and sometimes ferries may even be accompanied by small schools of dolphins.

---

griffon and Egyptian vultures and golden eagles. Seasoned bird of prey watchers stand a chance of seeing several other species. The ruins and excavations themselves harbour lizards and insects in abundance, and these fall prey to rock nuthatches which are perfectly at home on the stones and are the only birds you are likely to see actually walking down a rock face.

A surprising number of orchid species flower among the excavations at Delfí and colourful scrub flowers would soon invade from the surrounding land if left to their own devices. Among this aromatic cover, and also in the trees planted around the site, search for small songbirds such as warblers and sombre tits. An extremely good range of animal life can be found among the groves of olives and fruit trees in and around the village. More adventurous visitors should follow the zig-zag path which leads up the cliffs and eventually to the Levádhia plateau. Watch for crag martins and rock buntings on your way, as well as the colourful flowers growing on rock ledges and in crevices.

Parnassós

Snow-capped peaks and forested mountains within easy reach of Athens.

The fruits of Arbutus unedo, *the aptly named strawberry tree*

The olive

Olives have been cultivated for centuries if not millennia in most parts of lowland Greece and feature both in the cuisine and the history of the land. The fruit of the olive tree is a delightful food on its own but, more importantly, is a source of valuable oil. This is extracted from ripe, black olives, harvested in early autumn, traditionally in stone presses but nowadays using hydraulic presses. Groves of olives, characterised by their gnarled and twisted trunks and grey-green foliage, are a familiar sight in Greece. The trees are also havens for insects and nesting birds.

A griffon vulture scans the ground below for signs of a meal

Visitors to Delfí may like to linger a while in the area and explore the slopes of the Parnassós mountains more thoroughly. The range rises to an altitude of 2,457m at Liakoura but even at more modest elevations, an interesting range of plant and animal life can be found and observed. Compared to some of Greece's other mountain ranges, Parnassós is relatively easy to gain access to: a road leads from the village of Arákhova, on the Athens to Delfí road, taking you high into the mountains as it heads northwards.

Huge tracts of Greek fir forests dominate the lower slopes of Parnassós. Although comparatively few plants grow in the shade of the trees, roadside verges are often productive and the forests themselves are home to interesting birds such as crested tits and white-backed and black woodpeckers. Above the tree-line, low-growing alpine plants can be found and visitors should also keep an eye open for birds such as rock thrushes, alpine accentors and black redstarts.

PEACE AND QUIET

Mountain birds

For the most part, Greece is an extremely mountainous country with lowland regions restricted in the main to coastal districts. Not surprisingly, upland bird species are well represented in many parts. Several species of eagles and vultures can be seen, often in good numbers, at several of the historic sites set in rugged terrain. Smaller birds are also found at high altitudes and species such as alpine choughs and alpine accentors are habitually found close to the snow line.

Peloponnese

Wild and rugged terrain, rich in flowers and dry-country wildlife.
The Peloponnese (Pelopónnisos) is to all intents and purposes an island, connected to mainland Greece only by the narrow isthmus at Kórinthos (Corinth). It is a region of rugged, limestone hills much of which is inaccessible except on foot. Study the Peloponnese on a map and you will be struck by the long peninsulas stretching out into the sea: in outline, it is fancifully said to resemble the palmate leaf of a Mediterranean tree.
The village, Byzantine architecture and ruins at Mistra, near Spárti (Sparta) in the southern Peloponnese, is a popular spot for visitors. Of all the Greek sites of antiquity, this is surely one of the best for the visiting naturalist: colourful flowers can be found on and around the site and an excellent range of birds and insects also live here.
From as early as March and April, look for giant orchids and yellow bee orchids, as well as pinks, clovers, asphodels and brooms. Warblers, buntings and flycatchers are most noticeable in the spring. Many are just stopping off on migration but some stay to nest among the olive trees and Judas-trees that grow here. Mistra lies beside the route between Spárti and Kalámai. This road also passes through the Langarda gorge which is best explored from the village of Trípi. Watch the skies overhead for birds of prey. Many of the roads that criss-cross the passable sections of the Peloponnese offer spectacular views. Two in particular are worth mentioning and these are the route from Pátrai to Kalávrita and that from Trípolis to Spárti. Watch for birds of prey soaring overhead

The Mediterranean Sea

The coast of the Mediterranean is not the ideal for land-based marine biologists. Being relatively small in oceanic terms, and effectively land-locked, its tidal range is small, so there are few opportunities to study inter-tidal marine life and coastal birds are relatively scarce. Borrow a snorkel and mask, however, and a revelation will take place. Swim out just a few metres from the shore and you will discover seas teeming with life; rocky shores offer the best opportunities for study.

and, if you are visiting between April and June, stop periodically to explore roadside areas for flowers, insects and tortoises.

Mesolóngion
A haven for waterbirds and wetland wildlife.
Travel west along the northern shores of the Gulf of Corinth and you eventually come to Mesalóngion (Missalonghi), a town which is now bypassed by a new road. It is the focal point for a huge network of saline lagoons, some given over to fish production and others to salt. Large numbers of waterbirds can be found here throughout the year. In the spring, terns, plovers, avocets and black-winged stilts nest here and huge numbers of birds pass through on spring and autumn migration.

Ólimbos Óros (Mount Olympos)
Greece's highest mountain, rich in endemic flowers and mountain birds.
Although a considerable distance from Athens, plenty of visitors make a trip at least to the foothills of Mount Olympus. Even at comparatively low elevations, plantlife can be found in profusion and walkers can ramble against a backdrop of the snow-covered tops. Access is via the village of Litokhoron from where a road leads to the first of the Hellenic Alpine Club's mountain refuges; you reach the other refuges on foot as you make your ascent.

Cape Sounion at sunset, a scene epitomising the romantic nature of much of the Greek landscape

Practical

This section (with the yellow band) includes food, drink, shopping, accommodation, nightlife, tight budget, special events, etc

FOOD AND DRINK

Athens has a poor reputation for food, with much advice being given about avoiding tourist traps like the Plaka, yet it is perfectly easy to eat very well indeed, and at cheaper prices than in most other European capitals, whether in the Plaka or out of it. It is true that Greece does not have one of the great cuisines of the world, but visitors will still find that eating out in Athens, in a well chosen taverna, can be a fitting end to the day, with one unique feature: Greek atmosphere. Greeks enjoy their food, so why shouldn't the visitor?

The difference between the taverna and the generally slightly more up-market *estiatorio* can sometimes be no more than the name, but you could say that if it has tablecloths and proper wine glasses then it's an *estiatorio*, anything else, then it's a taverna. The 'anything else' is usually a paper or plastic sheet clipped into place as you sit

Making the ferry spick and span in Piraeus harbour

down, and cleared away again after the meal, with a small tumbler for your wine (although many Greeks drink beer or soft drinks with their meals). Greece is very casual, and while some of the more expensive restaurants do have a dress code, they are very few, diners normally dressing to suit themselves. It is quite possible to see diners in jeans being warmly welcomed in establishments that in some other countries would turn them away. The Greeks also love children, and this applies at mealtimes too. Meals are family occasions, and children dine with their families till late at night.

Something to watch out for is that Athenian eating places are not always all-year-round affairs. With typical Greek perversity it is not winter when your choice will be restricted, but summer. Many restaurants close in July and August, and others for longer summer periods, as owners turn their attentions to their other establishments on the Greek Islands, or visit relatives abroad. Dates vary and plans

PRACTICAL – FOOD AND DRINK

can change, so it is difficult to give precise information. Many also close on Sunday, so check before making a special journey to a restaurant.

Eating Habits

It is the Greek habit to eat late, taking lunch at perhaps 14.00hrs and dinner at 21.00hrs (but eating places will be open much earlier). Some dishes are prepared well in advance, however, the result being that your evening meal is lukewarm. This is not cause for complaint, it's simply the Greek way. If you like your food hot, choose a grill or fresh fish rather than moussaka.

It is rare that you would need to reserve a table in advance, unless dining at a popular restaurant on a Saturday evening. Telephone numbers for restaurants (under **Where to Eat**, pages 84–7) are only given where bookings are taken. You will see reserved tables from time to time, but the Greek way is more typically to turn up unannounced in large numbers and expect to be seated. If dining in the open air, extra tables can always be found from somewhere and all will be rearranged to suit the diners. If a place is full, simply wait and look hopeful. At the same time, there is no pressure on diners who have almost finished to give up their tables. By law, menus should show prices both with and without tax, and the two figures are usually shown side by side: you pay the higher. Prices are controlled by the Tourist Police, and should be openly

displayed. Menus are often in English and Greek, though there are exceptions so a phrase book is useful. In many tavernas it is normal to ask to go into the kitchen and see the day's dishes. You cannot judge a Greek eating place by looks, unless it shows obvious signs of neglect. The most basic place can serve the most wonderful food. Eat where the Athenians eat.

In a taverna a meal can be an unpredictable sequence of courses, less so in an *estiatorio*. Dishes come when they are ready, so a side-order of fried potatoes or salad may arrive at the start of a meal, a cooked starter later, and the main dish will arrive when it is ready. If this worries you, then you will have to adjust your ordering habits, requesting things as you want them. For dessert, the best plan is often to have a coffee and Greek-style cake at a nearby *zaharoplasteion* (patisserie).

What to Order

A good way to begin is with *mezedes* or *meze,* a selection of starters which can be substantial enough for a complete meal. It may include familiar dishes such as *taramosalata* (cod's roe pâté), *tzatsiki* (yoghurt, garlic and cucumber dip) and *melitzanosalata* (aubergine pâté).

Fish, which is expensive, is sold by weight. Choose the piece you want, asking for it to be weighed and priced beforehand – otherwise, if you ask, for instance, for a swordfish

steak you may get an enormous and costly portion (Greeks have big appetites). Swordfish (*xifias*) is common and delicious, while fried squid (*kalamaris/kalamarakia*) is popular as main course or starter. Other typical seafood is red mullet (*barbouni*), lobster (*astakos*) and whitebait (*maridhes*).

Fish and meat are often charcoal grilled. Try chicken (*kotopoulo*), lamb (*arni*) or pork (*hirino*), any of which can be served as *souvlaki*: skewered chunks, with or without pieces of tomato, onion and pepper. Most menus offer a limited choice of dishes suitable for

Souvlaki, *grilled meat on a skewer, is a popular dish*

vegetarians. Anything stuffed (tomatoes, peppers, aubergines, vine leaves) may or may not include minced meat , so ask the waiter. Otherwise there are *gigandes* (white beans), *koukia* (broad beans), *vriam* (ratatouille), *voureki* (courgette/potato/cheese pie) and a variety of salads such as *horiatiki* (referred to as Greek, peasant or country salad).

Desserts are limited, sticky and sweet, the most common being *baklava* (honey and nuts in pastry), *galaktoboureko* (custard pie) and *kataifi* (shredded wheat soaked in honey). Alternatives are usually ice-cream or fruit, frequently watermelon (*karpouzi*).

Drinks

The Greek aperitif is *ouzo*, an aniseed-flavoured drink like Pernod, served with a glass of water. Greeks tend to drink *ouzo* neat, with an occasional sip of water, though visitors may care to dilute the strong spirit with the water, which turns it milky. Alternatives such as vodka and gin are readily available too.

Greek wine (*krasi*) has even less of a reputation than Greek cuisine. *Aspro* is white, *mavro* red, *sero* dry and *gliko* sweet. The choice on most menus is limited to a few popular brands, with little to choose between them. *Retsina* is unique to Greece, a white wine strongly flavoured with pine resin from the barrels in which it was originally stored. Though not to everyone's taste, it complements the rather oily Greek food well. Greeks are not, as a rule, strong drinkers, often preferring fizzy drinks or a bottle of beer with their food. Beer is usually German lager-style, in bottles and cans, such as Amstel and Heineken, some brewed in Greece under licence. A few places serve draught beer, which is much more expensive.

After a meal, brandy is the favoured nightcap, usually the leading brand, Metaxa. The three-star type is a little rough, five-star palatable and seven-star smooth.

Where to Eat

In the Plaka

The greatest concentration of eating places is in the Plaka, and there are poor places as well as good ones. It is best to stick to recommendations, and a simple rule is never to eat anywhere where someone stands outside to entice you in. There are exceptions to this, but not many. Basement restaurants may not appeal in summer, but at other times they make safe bets. All three along Kidhathineon attract locals and other Athenians, and offer

limited menus, but inexpensive and well-cooked simple food, with wine from the barrel and a genuine Greek atmosphere. These are **To Ypogeio tis Plakas** (at No 10), **I Saita** (21) and **Bakalarakia** (41). The first two also have fine murals by local artist, George Savakis (see page 50).

Athenians also rate **Xynos** (moderate prices, open 20.00–02.00hrs, closed Sunday), tucked away since 1936 in the tiny alley of Angelou Geronta off Kidhathineon (tel: 322-1065). It looks not to have been decorated since it

opened, but that does not detract from the good simple dishes and lively nightly music. A famous but moderately-priced Athens eating place is the well-located **O Platanos** at Dioyenous 4. The smell from its grill fills the square around the ancient plane tree which gives the restaurant its name and shades the outdoor tables in midsummer (open daily except Sunday, from noon and from 20.00hrs). Round the corner is the slightly more sophisticated

Your selection of fish or seafood is cooked to order

PRACTICAL – FOOD AND DRINK

Aerides at Markou Avriliou 3 (tel: 322-6266). This café/restaurant opens for breakfast, lunch and dinner and serves everything from a coffee to a full meal. The dining room upstairs gives a magnificent view of the Tower of the Winds and Roman Agora, and daily specials include *agni youvetsi* (baked lamb) and baked eggplant with cheese. Opposite the Roman Agora's entrance is Eolou, with the **Five Brothers Restaurant** at No 3 (tel: 325-0088). This friendly place is open daily from 09.30–01.00hrs and has a very wide menu including a good variety of fixed-price three- and four-course meals. Specials might include octopus or a delicious baked aubergine with cheese and tomato. A visit to the kitchen is readily offered, and with a limited vegetarian menu and a smooth house wine, the result is enjoyable. Athens' only vegetarian restaurant is the **Eden** at Lysiou 12 (tel: 324-8858, open noon to midnight, closed Tuesday), in a large split-level dining room

with a rare (for Athens) 'no smoking' area. Its wide and reasonably-priced menu includes meat-free moussaka and specialities such as mushroom pie and *bureki* (mixed courgettes and potatoes topped with feta cheese). Delicious brown bread and fresh, non-Greek (and refilled) cups of coffee add to the pleasures. **Zorba's** at Lysiou 15 (tel: 322-6188) is more typically Plaka, open daily from 17.00hrs till late, and for Sunday lunch, when tables spread along the narrow street. There are specials such as lamb Zorba and various *saganaki* (fried cheese) dishes, and an eclectic décor, from the Mona Lisa to a pencil sketch which amusingly and accurately caricatures the two owners.

Outside the Plaka
Some of the best food in Athens is to be had at the other side of the Akropolis, at the unpretentious **Socrates' Prison** (Mitseon 20, tel: 922-3434),

Touting for custom in the Plaka

named for the owner not the philosopher. In fact their special salad would have fed the original Socrates in his prison for several days. Starters include mouthwatering aubergine croquettes, main courses are enterprising, such as beef roll stuffed with parsley, green pepper and aubergine, while desserts range from baked apple to home-made walnut cake. Moderate prices. For more formal meals, the expensive **Ta Nissia** at the Athens Hilton (tel: 725-0201) would be hard to beat, mixing international cuisine with Greek dishes: booking definitely recommended (open daily 19.30–00.30hrs, closed July–August). A recent venture is **G B Corner** at the Grande Bretagne Hotel, at the junction of Syntagma and Panepistimiou (tel: 323-0251). Though formal in style it is friendly in typical Greek manner, and the international menu does include several Greek dishes, such as lamb in a lemon sauce (tender meat, subtle sauce) and a Sunday buffet lunch. The equally pricey **Gerofinikas** is at Pindharou 10 (open 12.30–23.30hrs daily, tel: 363-6710/362-2719). This must be booked, and its menu is Greek Oriental-style. Chicken with pine kernels and currant pilaf could be served alongside a traditional *mouskari*: veal with vegetables, baked in a paper bag.

In nearby Kolonaki, the **18** restaurant is at Sovidias 51 (tel: 723-5561/7878). It moved from 18 Kolonaki Square 15 years ago but kept the name. It has an ambitious menu, with three different mushroom dishes among the starters, for example, and smoked salmon and Chateaubriand as well as Greek dishes such as veal in lemon sauce. A 'luxury' standard restaurant, with prices to match. Open Monday to Saturday, 13.00–02.00hrs.

Salamandra at Matzarou 3 (tel: 361-7927) specialises in Greek dishes, such as *saganaki* (fried cheese) and *spetzofai* (spicy sausage and pepper stew). Salads include a creamy Roquefort salad, with tasty brown bread and a good wine list. Not too expensive, the standard is high and makes it well worth finding this tiny side-street between the University and Likavitós. Also tucked away near by, but in complete contrast, is the traditional lunchtime *ouzerie*, **Apotsos**, in the arcade at Venizelou 10. One large square high-ceilinged room, the walls a mass of paintings, photos and old advertising slogans, Apotsos serves substantial 'tit-bits' to take with your *ouzo*: meatballs, sausages, grilled fish, salads. No fancy cooking, just simple food and a great Athens atmosphere.

For a bustling Greek night out visit **Barba Yannis** (E Benaki 94, tel: 330-0185) in Exarhia, an area of artists and students near the Archaeological Museum. Cooking is Greek basic – moussaka, beans, fish, *souvlaki* – the place buzzes with noise, perhaps with music, and diners queue for tables later in the evening even in midwinter. Cheap and cheerful.

SHOPPING

Athens is an adequate without being an exciting shopping city. Most quality shops for clothing and jewellery are concentrated in the desirable Kolonaki area, between the Parliament Building and Likavitós. Reasonably priced silver and gold items can be found, and leatherware is another good buy, from summer sandals to thick winter coats. Then, if you have the carrying capacity, there are woollen blankets, along with *flokati*, the Greek sheepskin rugs from the mountain regions.

For something that is recognisably Greek, try the shops attached to the various museums. These often stock art and craft items, as well as excellent reproductions of pieces from their own collections. Tapes of Greek music are good souvenirs, as are the worry-beads on sale in most tourist shops. Sponges from the islands are exported around the world, so are much cheaper when bought in Greece. Greek food and wine generally does not travel well, though some brand-name spirits are good bargains. Cooks should stock up on cheap virgin olive oil as well as honey, herbs and spices.

In the heart of the Plaka district you will find shops offering everything from the cheapest souvenir to expensive antiques. Many of the larger tourist shops seem from the outside to stock identical mass-produced goods, yet some do sell exclusive work by particular artists or craftsmen inside, particularly jewellery and ceramics.

One art at which many Greeks do excel is photography, and there are some fine ranges of picture postcards, and larger prints, of beautiful Greek scenes. There are many good, small art galleries too, for a more tasteful – and expensive – memory of Greece.

Arts

Some of the more interesting galleries exhibiting work by modern Greek artists (most of them in Kolonaki) include **Aegokeros**, Aristodimou 4; **Argo**, Merlin 8; **Athens Art Gallery**, Glykonos 4; **Desmos**, Akadhimias 28; **Medusa**, Xenokratous 7; **Maria Papadopoulou Gallery**, Xenokratous 33; **Skouffa Gallery**, Skouffa 4. **The**

Bargaining

Haggling is sometimes acceptable, especially in tourist areas such as the Plaka, where the shop owner often starts you off on the process anyway, by immediately quoting you a price less than the one on the ticket. He hopes to persuade you that you are getting a bargain, but the bold shopper will explore the possibility of the price coming down still further – it usually will. Jewellery and craft shops often have room for manoeuvre, although by no means as much as is common in the Middle East or North Africa.

The Plaka is the place to look for quality leather goods

Zoumboulakis Galleries at Kolonaki 20 and Kriezotou 7 also have foreign art, folk art, embroidery, antiques and jewellery for sale. There are many more, as well as a number of sculpture and ceramics studios, with some particularly attractive work in simple geometric forms at **Forum Hellas**, Kodrou 14.

Books
Several bookshops stock foreign language titles, and the limited amount of Greek fiction and non-fiction that has been translated into other languages. An enterprising series by the publishers **Kedros** offers 15 modern Greek novels in English, very cheap and hardly available outside Greece. **Compendium**, Nikis 28, has large second-hand and travel sections; **Deutsche Buchhandlung** is at Stadiou 10 and Omirou 4, and other German books at **Notos** (Omirou 15) and **Panitoglou** (Akadhimias 74); **Kaufman**, Stadiou 28, is good for French, German and Italian publications; **Pantelides** (Amerikis 11) and **Eleftheroudhakis** (Nikis 4) stock UK and US titles, as well as Greek; **Reymond's** at Voukourestiou 18 stocks books and journals in most foreign languages; and **I Folia tou**

Vivliou (The Booknest) at Venizelou 25 has a huge English-language stock.

Clothes

The Plaka is the place to go if you simply want some fun T-shirts, with more tasteful T-shirts and sweatshirts available at several of the museum shops. Kolonaki is the area for expensive fashion, male and female, but remember that several designers have chic outlets in some of the luxury hotels. See **Yanis Travassaros** in the Athens Hilton, and **Nikos and Takis** in the Astir Palace. There are also several long-established family firms which have been catering to the fur trade in Athens for generations, principally **Voula Mitszakou** at Mitropoleos 7, **Trahos** at Filellinon 7 and **Sistovaris** at Voulis 14, Ermou 4 and Venizelou 9.

Crafts

Many shops stock mundane craft items, but some quality goods can be found at specialists such as the **National Welfare Organisation**, Ipatias 6, with excellent kilims (woven rugs), ceramics, tapestries and copperware, many designed by Greek artists using folk or classical themes and made by women throughout the rural provinces of Greece. **Kokkinos** at Mitropoleos 3 is good for woollen rugs, as is the 'shop' on the steps at the junction of Pandhrossou and Kirikiou, which specialises in work from Metsovo in the Pindus Mountains. **The Centre for Hellenic Tradition** is at Pandhrossou 36 (see page 31).

For a more unusual type of craft see the puppetmakers, **Studio Kostas Sokaras**, at Adhrianou 25.

Food and Drink

The best place for either picnic lunches or something to bring home is naturally around the market area, near the meat and fish markets, with the nearby fruit and vegetable markets. These can be found along **Athinas**, which runs from Monastiráki metro north to Omonia. Shops here and in side-streets sell cheese, olives, olive oil, bread and fresh or pre-packed herbs and spices. If you want to take home some *ouzo*, *retsina* or Metaxa brandy, you will find it cheaper here than in the several drinks shops in the Plaka, though there won't be as wide a choice.

Icons

It is illegal to export antiques from Greece without permission, but modern icons in traditional style are still being produced in the religious shops that cluster in the streets south of Mitropoleos, notably Apollonos and Nikodimou.

Jewellery

Visit the **old silversmiths' quarter** of the city, on Leka and Praxitelous, for samples of work from old silversmith families from Ioannina, the capital of the Epirus region and renowned for this craft. Here you can also find anything that can possibly be produced from silver or gold, from guitars to the most ornate picture-frames imaginable. For more refined tastes, several shops on **Voukourestiou** offer elegant jewellery. Near by are two of Athens' most famous jewellers, with **Lalounis** at Venizelou 6 and **Zolotas** at Venizelou 10. At the other end of the price – and social – scale, young people sell hand-made jewellery, mainly silver and turquoise, along Areos, south of Monastiráki, near the Sunday morning flea-market.

Junk

The **flea-market** west of Monastiráki is open every day, although many more shops only open their shutters on Saturday and Sunday. Sunday morning is the big occasion, when the choice ranges from genuine antiques to curios to cloths spread on the ground and covered with a few objects that it is hard to imagine anyone wanting to buy. Also on Sunday morning is the less touristy but no less frenetic flea-market in Piraeus, off Ippodamou, very close to the metro station.

Music

Records, cassettes and CDs are slightly cheaper in Athens than in some cities, and there is a good choice of modern music at the two large branches of **Metropolis**, at the Omonia end of Venizelou. Both also stock Greek music, as do many souvenir shops. There are several music shops – and one traditional musical instrument shop – in the flea-market, but the place to go for traditional Greek music is the well-stocked shop at the **Museum for Greek Musical Instruments** (see page 40).

Take home some local tipple

ACCOMMODATION

Athens has a wide range of excellent mid-range hotels, many conveniently placed in and around the Plaka district. They give easy access to the Acropolis, many museums, good shopping and the widest choice of eating places, only a few minutes' walk from Syntagma Square and fashionable Kolonaki. It is far easier for the average visitor to find a good and affordable central hotel in Athens than it is in most other European capitals.

Accommodation is inspected regularly by the Tourist Police and graded according to a range of criteria. The top grade is Luxury, the rest go from A to E class. The grade affects the prices, which are fixed by law – though this is not to say that an unofficial price may not be sometimes agreed. Prices are per room not per person, though a single traveller may be offered a discount on a double room, if available. Prices should be displayed in the room, though this is not always adhered to, and in any case price lists can be confusing. Prices vary with the season, last year's list may not have been updated, and prices might be quoted with or without taxes, and with or without breakfast. In the unlikely event of your being grossly overcharged, report the matter to the Tourist Police. They have the power to close

Arriving without Accommodation

If you are arriving by air, the Greek National Tourist Organisation has an information desk at the East Terminal (tel: 970-2395) and can advise. In Piraeus, their office is in the EOT building on the Zea Marina harbour (tel: 413-5716). If these are closed, head for central Athens, taking the airport bus to Syntagma or the metro from Piraeus to Monastiráki. Both destinations are on the edge of the Plaka, where there are many excellent inexpensive hotels. There are three on Kodrou alone, and if these are full the owners will direct you to others near by. In any case it is difficult to walk in Athens with baggage for more than five minutes without being asked if you are looking for a hotel. Here common sense must prevail. Some of the offers will be genuine, though naturally you will be guided to a friend's or relative's hotel. It is unlikely you will be led down a dark alley and mugged, though there are confidence tricksters as in all cities. Ask the person the name of the hotel, where it is, how far it is and how much it will cost. If the answers are vague ('come with me, I show you, not far'), it is best to stay where you and ask a policeman or shopkeeper for help. It is better to ask a shopkeeper, who knows the area and is known, rather than rely on an unknown stranger in the street.

PRACTICAL – ACCOMMODATION

Old-world splendour in the foyer of the Grande Bretagne hotel

establishments down, and few hotel owners would risk that against a short-term gain from a tourist.

Luxury hotels are of the same standard as anywhere else in the world, A and B class generally have all or most of their rooms with private facilities, C class hotels can be anything, while in D and E class you should not expect private facilities and these are mainly low budget options. The grading system is only a general guideline to standards. For example, the Adonis and Electra Palace (see page 95), are both A class hotels within 100 metres of each other, yet the latter has many more facilities and is three times as costly as the former – though both are good for their price. It is perfectly acceptable to ask to see a room before committing

yourself. Foreign visitors must surrender their passports until the details have been entered in the hotel's records. This can take anything from one minute to several days.

Luxury

Astir Palace, Platia Sindagma (tel: 364-3112), has a marble staircase and mosaic walls, making elegant surroundings for its luxurious facilities.

Athenaeum Inter-Continental, Syngrou 89-93 (tel: 902-3666; fax: 921-7653). The most expensive hotel in Athens with rooms ranging from the 'ordinary' (marble floors, desks, marbled bathrooms) to huge private suites.

Athens Hilton, Vasilissis Sofias 46 (tel: 725-0201; fax: 721-

Somewhere quiet to stay in the Plaka: the Acropolis House hotel

3110), has a courtyarded entrance where airline offices and banks surround gnarled olive trees. Its marbled interior is spectacular to see, all its rooms have city views, and its restaurants and swimming-pool are not the least of its attractions.

Divani Palace Acropolis, Parthenonos 19-23 (tel: 922-9650; fax: 921-4993), has very high standards, a huge and welcoming reception area, swimming-pool, all rooms with balconies, many with views of the Acropolis or the Pnyx.

Grande Bretagne, Platia Sindagma (tel: 323-0251; fax: 322-8034), an old-fashioned distinguished hotel boasting past guests as notable as Sir Winston Churchill and Richard Strauss. It was once an annexe to the Royal Palace, but is now modernised and all rooms have every facility, some overlooking a flowered inner courtyard, others viewing Syntagma Square (through sound-proof windows).

NJV Meridien, Platia Sindagma (tel: 325-5301), the smallest and newest of the luxury hotels, with 182 rooms, some upper ones boasting Acropolis views and all having satellite TV, mini-bars and direct-dial telephones with bathroom extensions.

A/B Class

Acropolis House, Kodrou 6-8 (tel: 322-2344). A small and pleasant family-run hotel, not all rooms *en suite*.

Adonis, Kodrou 3 (tel: 3249-737). Typical of the Plaka hotels, in a quiet pedestrianised street, with rooftop bar/breakfast room looking out at the Acropolis. Extremely helpful staff, well-furnished rooms.

Athenian Inn, Haritos 22 (tel: 7238-097). In the smart Kolonaki district. Some rooms look out on Likavitós, and are pleasingly furnished in traditional Greek-village style.

Electra, Ermou 5 (tel: 322-3222; fax: 322-0310). On busy Ermou and drab outside, but inside is a surprisingly attractive hotel, all rooms with TV and mini-bars and extremely comfortably furnished.

Electra Palace, Nikodhimou 18 (tel: 324-1401). With rooftop swimming-pool and roof garden, and very well appointed rooms, this is one of the best hotels on the edge of the Plaka.

The Lycabette, Valaoritou 6 (tel: 363-3514), is hidden away in a pedestrianised side-street, a welcome retreat in central Athens, near Kolonaki and Syntagma. Good facilities, inexpensive.

Olympic Palace Hotel, Filelinon 16 (tel: 323-7611). Very reasonably priced for its central location, between Plaka and National Gardens, bright and modern rooms.

C/D Class

Aphrodite, Apollonos 21 (tel: 323-4357), is one of the better budget hotels, central, and upper rooms even have an Acropolis view.

Hermes, Apollonos 19 (tel: 323-5514). A small, busy hotel, good for its price-range.

Nefeli, Yperidou 16 (tel: 3228-044), quietly located, a small family-run hotel with pleasant rooms.

Budget

Athens Youth Hostel, Kypselis 57 (822-5860). Slightly out of the centre, but with the Victoria metro not too far away. Reasonable standard.

Athens Connection, Ioulianou 20 (tel: 822-4592). Youth hostel with good facilities, close to Victoria metro and National Archaeological Museum.

Hotel Tempi, Eolou 29 (tel: 321-3175), clean but basic, getting close to hostel prices, no rooms have private WC but some have showers. Friendly owners, pleasant central location.

XEN (YWCA), Amerikis 11 (tel: 362-6180). Good facilities, if you don't mind the communal bathroom. One double room for married couples. There is no YMCA hostel in Athens.

CULTURE, ENTERTAINMENT AND NIGHTLIFE

For Athenians, a night out starts late and finishes late. However, concerned about an increase in teenage drinking and an on-going problem of people catching up on their sleep at work – and even children falling asleep at school through too many late nights – the Greek government cracked down. In 1994 they introduced legislation

PRACTICAL – ENTERTAINMENT

requiring establishments to close no later than 02.00hrs. The individualistic Greek people do not take kindly to being told what to do, and the more enterprising of them are finding ways around this. The law does not apply at sea, so boats are hired for all-night cruises, nor does it apply in travel terminals, hence the sudden popularity of the café at the main railway station.

This situation is in a state of flux, so those seeking a very late night out should check the latest circumstances. For those who are normally in bed by 02.00hrs anyway, Athens still has plenty to offer, ranging from classical drama, through traditional and modern music to plate-smashing in tavernas. Even this last custom has been made illegal now, except for a few places where a licence is held allowing the smashing of unglazed pottery. Join in if you feel like it, but the cost of the crockery will be added to your bill.

If you prefer slightly more sophisticated entertainment than smashing a saucer, the events to watch out for are those under the umbrella of the **Athens Festival**, which takes place each year from late June to September. There are concerts, both modern and classical, though the main emphasis is on drama. Greece is, after all, the birthplace of European theatre, and performances of plays by Sophocles, Euripedes and the other great names in Greek drama are prominent. These take place mainly at the

Herodes Atticus Theatre below the Acropolis, but also at weekends at Epidhavros (Epidaurus), with transport from Athens being organised to coincide. The journey is likely to provide as much drama and entertainment as any performance. Greek National Tourist Organisations abroad can provide a programme of events, as can most hotels and travel operators in Greece. To

Dora Stratou Dance Theatre

Dora Stratou spent her life studying and helping to preserve the many traditional Greek dances which exist in great variety throughout the mainland and islands. She amassed a collection of recordings, books and an estimated 3,000 dance costumes, as well as founding a dance school and dance troupe, which first performed in 1953. She died in 1988, but this theatre keeps her memory alive with nightly performances from 1 June to 30 September. It is officially the Filopappou Theatre (Théatro Filopápou) and is located at the foot of the Pnyx, being signposted from the entrance on Apostolou Pavlou, near the foot of the southern entrance to the Acropolis. Shows are held at 22.15hrs nightly, with extra shows at 20.15hrs on Wednesday and Sunday. The very cheap tickets can be bought at the entrance, at the Dora Stratou Foundation, Scholiou 8 in the Plaka, or booked (tel: 324-4395).

book, though, you need to contact the Festival Box Office, Stadhiou 4, Athens (tel: 322-1459/3111), whose opening hours are Monday to Friday, 08.30–13.30hrs and 18.00–20.30hrs. Tickets can also be bought at event venues. To find out about other events in Athens, read the English language newspapers *Athens News* and *Greek Weekly News*, the weekly listings guide *Athenscope* or the monthly *Athenian*, available at any newsagent or kiosk, or the Greek language *Athinorama*.

Cinema

Athens has a tradition of open-air cinemas; while some still function, many in or near the city centre have been forced to close, as their high rents were not covered by a few months of summer opening. One that remains is the **Ciné Paris** at Kidhathineon 22 (tel: 322-5745). Others will be improvised on

land used for car parking during the day. You should go mainly for fun, not for quiet attention to the film: Greeks talk, walk and eat throughout a show, and late-night performances will in any case have the soundtrack turned down to avoid disturbing residents.

In the more conventional cinemas, foreign films are widely shown in their original language with Greek subtitles. *Athenscope* lists over 50 indoor cinemas, mostly in central Athens and Piraeus and mostly showing the latest Hollywood movies, with several French titles and a note of the few films which have been dubbed into Greek. Classic films can be seen each Saturday at 18.00hrs at the **Hadjikyriakos-Ghika Cinema Museum**, Kriezotou 3 (tel: 362-6266).

Have a pre-dinner drink in a traditional ouzerie like this one

Theatre and Classical Concerts

Apart from classical drama at the Athens Festival, there is little of theatrical interest for the non-Greek speaker. Concerts and dance performances abound, though. The **Lykabettos Theatre** (tel: 322-1459) is below the summit of Likavitós and has mainly visiting contemporary musicians, while more classical repertoires can be found at venues such as the **Megaron** or **Athens Concert Hall** (tel: 729-0391), at the junction of Vasilissis Sofias and Kokkalis, the **National Opera** in the

Athenian theatre with a production of My Fair Lady

Olympia Theatre at Akadhimias 59 (tel: 361-2461), the **Gloria Theatre** at Ippokratou 7 (tel: 362-6702), and the **National Theatre**, Ayou Konstandinou 20 (tel: 522-3241).

Traditional and Modern Music

As with restaurants, some clubs close in the summer, and some close for one or even two nights during the week, doubtless to allow staff and customers time to recover. You should also be prepared for the fact that Greek music clubs, while great fun, can also be expensive compared to other entertainment in the city. Allow a few thousand drachma for a few drinks.

Most tavernas featuring **bouzouki music** and/or dancing are, inevitably, in the Plaka district and don't start much before 22.00hrs. Booking is advised. Try the long-established **Dionysos** at Lysiou 7 (tel: 322-7589), **Palea Taverna Kritikou** round the corner at Mniskleos 24 (tel: 322-2809), **Yeros tou Morea** at Mniskleos 27 (tel: 322-1753) and **Kalokerinos** at Kekropos 10 (tel: 323-2054). There are a number of *rembétika* **clubs**, featuring the more modern urban blues music (see page 40), such as **Frankosyrianni** at Arahovis 57 (tel: 360-0693) and **Taximi** at Issavron 29 (tel: 363-9919), both in Exarhia, a lively night-time area north of Likavitós. Or if you want to listen to music in the meat market, the **Stoa Athanaton** is a renovated warehouse right in its heart, at Sofolkeous 19 (tel: 321-4362).

For more wide-ranging jazz and blues, including western music, favourite places with Athenians include **Blue Velvet** at Ermou 16 (tel: 323-9047), **French Quarter** in the Neapoli district, at Mavromichali 78 (tel: 645-0758), the very popular **Half Note** at Fthiotidos 68 (tel: 644-9236) – though this is slightly out of the centre, in the Ambelokipi district – and the rather smart basement club, **Jazz Club 1920**, at Ploutarchou 10, Kolonaki (tel: 721-0533).

WEATHER AND WHEN TO GO

Athens has visitors all year round, although fewer in the December/February period when it can be cold and wet. However, it can also be be mild and boast blue skies, making an out-of-season visit to a normally packed Acropolis a genuine pleasure. The average temperature at this time of year is about 14°C, with a chance of a few wet days per month, so it is a gamble. In March/May and October/November you should take something warm to wear in the evenings, but for the main part of the summer the wise visitor travels light. Any cover-up clothing then is only likely to be needed if visiting monasteries and churches, where bare legs and bare shoulders might be considered disrespectful. In August there have been heatwaves several times in recent years, sending the average summer

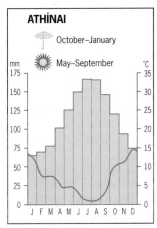

temperature of 30°C soaring to the 40°C mark. In Athens this can mean intense discomfort, and a noticeable increase in air pollution. It is a period to be avoided if at all possible. You would have to be very unlucky to experience more than the occasional day of rain if travelling between about April and September.

HOW TO BE A LOCAL

Sitting in a café for an hour or so, nursing a Greek coffee, will give a glimpse of ordinary Athenian life. Ask for a *metrio*, a medium, with just a little sugar to counteract the bitterness of the strong Greek coffee. *Sketo* is sugar-free, and *gliko* well sweetened. Greek coffee is served with a glass of water, for cleansing the palate.

Eat in the tavernas where the locals eat. Mealtimes are important Greek social occasions, especially Saturday evenings and Sunday lunchtimes. Watching a Greek family at a meal is a pleasure in itself, and you are sure to be in a place where food, service and value are all good.

Travel by bus, trolley or metro, if only once, though try to avoid the rush-hour – there are some experiences of local living best avoided! Many Athenians make the 90-minute sunset trip out to Cape Sounion and back on the bus – so join them (see page 65).

Visit the Sunday morning flea-market in either Piraeus or Monastiráki, when it seems that half of Athens is thronging the streets looking for a bargain.

Visit the street markets too – the Friday market in Xenokratous, Saturday morning along Kallidhromiou, and the daily flower market around Platia Ayia Irini.

CHILDREN

The Greeks are extremely tolerant of children and their exuberance, as will be evident if you visit a museum at the same time as a school party – a regular occurrence. The same tolerance applies in restaurants, where children in a group will often be given their own table, alongside their parents. If you are travelling with young children, you need not

therefore be embarrassed if they become a little fractious. You are far more likely to receive sympathy than disapproval.

While Athens is not the best city for children, with its wealth of ancient sites, there are places they will enjoy. **The Museum of Greek Musical Instruments** allows them to put on headphones and listen to the exhibits, while the **Greek Folk Art Museum** runs workshops – including some in English – teaching children traditional crafts. In the National Gardens there is a **Children's Library**, which has books and games in English and French as well as Greek, and of course with the

Youngsters letting off steam in the National Gardens

chance to meet and play with Greek children too.

Small mobile **amusement parks** are an *ad hoc* feature of Athens, so watch out for any in parks and on waste land, or take a trip out to the beaches around the popular resort of Glifádha. Children may be less bothered than adults about being under the airport flight path there. Smaller **playgrounds** can be found dotted around the city, with one in the National Gardens, another pleasantly situated in the grounds of Likavitós, near the Genadios Library.

TIGHT BUDGET

Athens is ideal for those on a budget, being one of the cheapest capitals in Europe, but the following few tips can make it cheaper still.

● Take the cheap and regular bus to and from the airport, or the metro to and from Piraeus, rather than a taxi.

● Throughout Greece, most sites and public museums have free admission on one day of the week, which is usually Sunday. In Athens there are a few places which are free on a different day, so check. Try to visit the two most expensive attractions, the Acropolis and National Archaeological Museum, on Sunday.

● The views from the Pnyx and the top of Likavitós are both free – though take your own food and drink to the latter: its cafés are *not* free.

● Avoid organised excursions. There are very few places that cannot be reached cheaply by public transport.

● When dining out, watch where the locals eat, in

You can eat cheaply at a souvlaki *stall in the Plaka*

particular priests and servicemen. Likely to be on a tight budget themselves, they can usually be relied on to find the best value-for-money taverna.

● Snacks such as cheese (*tiropitakia*) or spinach (*spanakopites*) pies are cheap ways of filling up, or buy picnic food in the market and eat lunch in the National Gardens.

● It's cheaper to change cash or travellers' cheques at a post office rather than a bank, but if you have a specific type of travellers' cheque then look for an office of that company, where commission may be waived altogether.

● Fish is the most expensive meal, and is normally sold by weight. Go in the kitchen and choose a specific piece, and ask for it to be weighed and priced for you so that you know what you're paying.

● The most expensive salad is the ubiquitous Greek or country salad (*horiatik*), with olives, feta cheese and other trimmings, so choose a cheaper tomato (*domatosalata*) or tomato and cucumber salad (*angour domata*).

● *Retsina* is the cheapest drink by far, but be sure to ask for a small bottle of a brand like Kourtaki or you may be given a more upmarket type at an upmarket price.

● The Greek system of grading hotels is only a guide. Some 'B' and even 'C' class hotels provide everything you want at half the cost of an 'A' class, so ask to see a room before committing yourself to it. See also **Camping** (page 111).

SPECIAL EVENTS

January
New Year's Day is celebrated as the Feast of St Basil, with services in churches, where you may see people offering the specially baked bread, *vassilopitta*: Basil bread. 6 January is **the Epiphany**, when it is a tradition for priests to bless baptismal fonts, and a good chance to see inside churches that are sometimes otherwise locked.

February/March
The **Carnivals** of Mardi Gras or Shrove Tuesday are not great celebrations, though in Athens you may find impromptu music sessions in the streets. It is also traditional for children to dress up (as anything from nuns to witches) and for them to hit people on the head with plastic hammers. The Plaka district becomes packed with Athenians. 25 March is **Independence Day**, celebrating the start of the revolt against Turkish domination and naturally important to the Athenians as it led to Athens becoming the modern nation's capital. There are speeches and celebrations in Syntagma Square.

May/June
May Day, 1 May, is when you may see the traditional workers' parades, while families often take a day out from Athens for family picnics and flower-gathering. The flowers are plaited into wreaths and hung on doors until 24 June, the **Feast of St John the Reaper**, when they are burnt, as summer has safely arrived.

PRACTICAL – SPECIAL EVENTS

Easter

The biggest single event in the Greek calendar is Easter, which is much more important than Christmas in the Orthodox Church. It is a movable feast that only coincides with the western church's Easter celebrations once every few years. As Easter Sunday normally falls somewhere between mid-April and early May, it can be a wonderful time to visit Athens, with the arrival of warm weather, not too many crowds, and the moving and colourful religious festivities to be enjoyed as well.

The Easter rituals begin in the week leading up to Good Friday; churches are filled with glorious floral decorations, children call on houses in the neighbourhood, distributing flowers and singing songs, and the bier which is to carry Christ's body through the streets on Good Friday is magnificently decorated. This procession takes place late in the evening after a service, and visitors need feel no inhibitions about joining the walkers. Occasions like this will make you realise that Athens, though a city, is actually a collection of small communities.

On Easter Saturday evening the main Easter service takes place, culminating at midnight with a brief extinguishing of all the lights, inside and outside the church. After a pause the priest will appear in the church with a lighted candle or taper, lighting the candle held by the nearest one of the congregation, who will in turn light other candles, till the church glows with illuminated faces. Then comes the priest's announcement: *Christos Anesti* ('Christ is risen') and the congregation's response: *Alithos Anesti* ('He is risen indeed'). The joyful news is celebrated by the return of lights everywhere and by the throwing of fireworks in the streets.

A wonderful viewpoint is from the Chapel of Ayios Yeoryios at the top of Likavitós, looking down on much of the city and watching for flickering candlelight as Athenians walk home from the city churches, trying to keep their candle flame lit in order to take it over the threshold and bring good fortune for the rest of the year. Some families will now have a meal of *magaritsa*, the traditional Easter soup of rice, lemon and lamb offal.

Sunday is a family day, with a morning service followed by a huge Sunday lunch, when the rest of the lamb is eaten. Easter bread is also eaten, and you will see red Easter eggs, which are simply hard-boiled eggs painted red. The traditional game is to knock the eggs against each other until only one uncracked egg is left. There will be other festivities, sometimes a communal evening meal with traditional dancing, and at this time locals will be especially pleased to see visitors joining them in their celebrations of rebirth and renewal.

July/August
In Athens summer brings the annual **Athens Festival**: see pages 96–7 for details. From July to mid-September is the very popular **Dafní Wine Festival**: see page 66 for details of the Dafní Monastery on the outskirts of Athens. Tickets for the festival are available from the Festival Box Office at Stadiou 4 (tel: 322-1459).
15 August is the **Feast of the Assumption of the Blessed Virgin Mary** (*Apokimisis tis Panayias*). On this day Greeks everywhere make an effort to return to their home village, and ferries to the islands are often full. It is not a good time to be travelling to or from Athens speculatively, though the city

Independence Day procession, one of the events of 25 March

on this day will be noticably quiet. The Feast will be celebrated at those churches named for the Virgin Mary: the Panayias.

October
After the many feasts throughout the summer months, there is a slight pause for breath before the rejoicing of 28 October, known as **Ohi Day**. This commemorates the day when the Greek leader, General Metaxas, gave a one-word response of *Ohi* (No) to an ultimatum from Mussolini in 1940 that his troops be allowed to pass through Greece. (In fact

Sailing boats at Piraeus

his response was longer, and in French at that, but why spoil a good story?) Syntagma again is the focal point, but with school and military parades throughout the city.

December

The Greek year winds down with **Christmas and New Year's Eve**, though these are not as important to the Greeks as is Easter.

SPORT

Football is the Greek obsession, with two great rival teams in the city. In Athens itself the team is Panathinaikos, their ground being on Alexandhras, at the junction with Kyriakou. Olympiakos of Piraeus have their home at the Karaiskaki Stadium, visible from the Faliro metro station, one stop before Piraeus. Matches are on Sunday afternoons, with some midweek games, so check the *Athens News* and similar publications for current fixtures.

If you cannot survive without **golf,** you will find an 18-hole public course at Glifádha on the outskirts of Athens (tel: 894-6820). Failing that, book the Golf Suite at the Athenaeum Inter-Continental Hotel (tel: 902-3666), which has its own indoor putting green.

There is, rather surprisingly for a large city, no shortage of clubs catering for **horseback riding.** These include the **Athens Riding Club** (tel: 661-1088), the **Hellenic Riding Club** (681-2506), and two in the suburb of Varybobi: the **Tatoi**

Riding Club (tel: 801-4513) and the **Varybobi Riding Club** (tel: 801-9912). **Horse racing** can be seen at the Hippodrome Stadium (tel: 363-1745) near the Faliro metro station. Meetings are usually held on Monday, Wednesday and Friday, from 14.30hrs in winter and from 18.00hrs in summer.

For information about **sailing** in the waters near Athens, contact the **Greek Sailing Federation** at Xenofondhos 15a, (tel: 323-5560/6813). Also in Athens is the **Greek Windsurfing Association**, at Filellinon 7 (tel: 323-0068/0330). Facilities are available for windsurfing and other **watersports** at some of the resorts along the coast. Athens has no public **swimming**-baths, but pools are open to the public – at a price –

at the Hilton and Inter-Continental hotels. The whole coast from Piraeus east towards Cape Sounion – the Apollo Coast – is given over to a series of bathing 'resorts'. However, the water is heavily polluted near Piraeus, the best beaches at Glifádha are directly under the airport flight path, and the beaches beyond that are not very good. None of this deters Athenian swimmers in the slightest.

Tennis is quite popular, with details about clubs and public courts available from the **EFOA Association**, Omirou 8 (tel: 323-0412), or the headquarters of the **Athens Tennis Club** (tel: 923-2872).

If you want to swim there are coastal resorts not far from the city

Directory

This section (with the biscuit-coloured band) contains day-to-day information, including travel, health and documentation.

Contents

Arriving
By Air

There are scheduled flights to Athens from most countries, and the national airline, Olympic, covers most routes alongside major airlines such as Qantas, KLM, Virgin Atlantic, British Airways, Aer Lingus, Air Canada, Delta, Singapore Airlines and others. Olympic uses the western terminal at Ellinikon International Airport in Athens while all other airlines use the eastern terminal, both terminals being in the eastern seaside suburb of Glifádha (10km southeast of the city

Byzantine icon. The style is virtually unchanged today

centre), just five minutes' drive apart. An hourly shuttle bus service runs between them from 08.30 to 20.30hrs, or you can take a taxi.

Taxis are also the quickest way into central Athens, but can prove expensive for the unwary. As with every major airport, not all taxi drivers are honest. Agree the fare before setting off (it should be about 1,000 drachma into Athens), or insist that the meter is on. It should have a figure '1' illuminated. If it shows a figure '2', double fare is being charged, only allowed between midnight and 05.00hrs or if travelling outside the city boundaries, which does not apply to the airport. Fares of five and ten times the right amount are sometimes demanded – and paid. Otherwise blue and yellow Express Buses, which leaves from the stop directly outside each terminal building, provide a cheap and easy alternative. They operate to and from the terminals every 30 or 40 minutes, direct to the centre of Athens with stops at Syntagma and Omonia Squares (the service for one terminal does not stop at the other). Buy your ticket from the driver but time-stamp it in the machine behind him. A similar bus service goes between both terminals and Piraeus, but not via central Athens. There is no metro or train station near by.

There are (minimal) banking and shopping facilities in both terminals, and offices for major car rental companies, such as Hertz, Avis and Budget.

By Sea

There are many ferry services in and out of Piraeus, the port of Athens and one of the busiest in the Mediterranean. Some of the major routes include Venice in Italy, Istanbul in Turkey, Limassol and Larnica in Cyprus, Haifa in Israel and Port Said and Alexandria in Egypt. Piraeus is a typical port, full of life though some of it not the kind the average visitor may wish to see. Its metro station links with central Athens, the most convenient stops being Monistiráki for the Plaka, or Omonia Square. The service runs from 05.30 to midnight. Buses are not particularly

useful: the local (green) bus, route 040, is not conveniently located and the Express Bus, route 19, runs roughly every hour from Piraeus to western and eastern air terminals but not to the city centre. A taxi to the centre should cost about 1,000 drachma, but heed the warnings in the 'By Air' section.

By Road

The most popular route to Athens from western Europe is via Italy and across the Adriatic by ferry, and then a very scenic drive across central Greece to the capital. The main highway through the former Yugoslavia has been closed for some time, requiring a diversion to the east towards Budapest and Belgrade. This is the route favoured by coach services, including members of the Eurolines network which covers most European countries.

By Rail

To travel by rail from northern Europe to Athens takes about three days and costs almost as much as a scheduled flight (unless a student, under-26 or other discount applies).

Entry Formalities

For a stay of up to 90 days (180 days for Britons, 60 days for New Zealanders), citizens of the USA, Canada, Australia, the European Union and most non-EU European countries require only a valid passport to enter Greece. To extend your stay, apply in good time to the Aliens' Bureau (*Ipiresia Allodhapon*) at Halkokondhili 9, open Monday–Friday 08.00–13.00hrs.

Camping

The most convenient of the dozen or so sites around Athens are both in the pleasant northern suburb of Kifisiá, well-served by the metro to central Athens and Piraeus. **Camping Akropolis** (tel: 807-5253) is a B-grade and **Camping Nea Kifisiá** (tel: 807-5579) an A-grade on the A (excellent) to C (satisfactory) scale monitored by the tourist authorities. Other A-grade sites are the **Karabateas** (tel: 598-1150) on the main road near the monastery in Dafní and the **Vula** (tel: 895-2712) at Alkyonidon 2 in the suburb of Vola. For further information contact **Association Greek Camping**, Solonos 102, Athens 10680 (tel: 362-1560). An International Camping Carnet is useful, though not normally requested. Sites are usually open from April to October. Unofficial camping is illegal.

Moving on from Piraeus

Car Rental

Rates in Greece are expensive. Legally an International Driving Licence is required except for those holding a UK, German, Belgian or Austrian driving licence, although in practice other European, American and Australasian licences are accepted. Minimum age varies from 21 to 25, according to the hire company. You are advised to rent from a recognised company: the rates may be higher but the car will be safer. Most major rental companies have desks at the airport, and in central Athens most offices are together on Singrou, almost opposite the Temple of Olympian Zeus: Budget (No 8, tel: 921-4771), Speedo (No 8, tel: 922-6102), Hertz (No 12, tel: 922-0102), Thrifty (No 24, tel: 922-1211), Eurodollar (No 29, tel: 922-9672), Just Rent A Car

(No 43, tel: 923-9104) and Autorent (No 94, tel: 923-2514). Avis is at Amalias Sofias 46-8 (tel: 322-4951).

The insurance coverage insisted on by law and included in standard agreements is generally not adequate should there be a serious accident. You are strongly advised to add Collision Damage Waiver (CDW) insurance, at a small extra cost (rental companies will probably try to sell you this anyway). This gives you full insurance cover irrespective of responsibility for an accident.

Crime

Greece is one of the safest countries in Europe, and very few visitors become victims of crime. In Athens, muggings and other such offences are occasional rather than common happenings, and the average visitor, if not wandering unknown streets late at night, is unlikely to be affected.

Customs Regulations

The normal duty free allowances apply if arriving from other EU countries (non-EU figures in brackets): 300 (200) cigarettes or 75 (50) cigars or 150 (100) cigarillos or 400 (250) grams of tobacco; one and a half litres (one litre) of spirits or five (two) litres of wines, sparkling wines or

Omonia Square: only masochists and Athenians drive in Athens

liqueurs; 75 (50) grams of perfume and 37.5 (25) centilitres of toilet water. Also you can bring in gifts to the value of 137,000 drachma or, for a single item, to a maximum of 77,500 drachma (but only a total of 10,500 drachma from non-EU countries).

Cats and dogs require health and rabies inoculation certificates from a veterinary authority in the country of origin dated not less than six days or more than 12 months (cats six months) from the date of arrival. Importation of antiquities and works of art is permitted, but they must be declared and the value stated if they are to be re-exported It is forbidden to export antiquities and works of art found in Greece. The allowances for exporting goods vary with the destination so check this before departure. For currency, see **Money Matters**, page 117.

Disabled Visitors

Greece is not the easiest of countries for disabled visitors. While most Greeks are cheerfully helpful, some also prefer to look away, and hotel, public transport and other facilities lag behind the times. The Athenaeum Inter-Continental is one hotel which has rooms specially adapted for the disabled. Access to some of the sites will be difficult if not impossible. Assume nothing and check everything in advance. A useful organisation to contact is the **National Association of Rehabilitation for the Handicapped**, Odhos Hassias, Nea Liossia, KA 1322 Athens.

See Athens in style – but at a price

Driving

Greece has one of the worst road safety records in the world, with seven deaths per day, and Athens is not for the faint-hearted driver. The traffic is so congested in the centre that entry of cars is restricted daily to even number-plates one day, odd numbers the next. On very smoggy days, the restricted zone is enlarged so that drivers must complete their journeys by public transport or taxi. Drivers need to know their way round the city, as signposting is limited and diversions frequent.

If your visit is confined to Athens, a car is unlikely to be needed, with most of the main sites being within easy walking distance of the centre. Virtually all the popular places that one

might wish to visit on excursions are accessible on either public transport, by going on organised day trips or by hiring a taxi for a few hours. To avoid needlessly driving in the city centre, consider picking up a hire car at the airport and leaving it there at the end of the hire period. The airport bus to the city centre is quick, frequent and cheap.
If you do decide to drive, then the speed limit is 50kph (31mph) in built-up areas, 80kph (49mph) outside built-up areas and 100kph (62mph) on dual carriageways and motorways. Do not expect motorways of international standard. Seat belts must be worn where fitted, and you must carry a warning triangle, fire extinguisher and first-aid kit. Any accident causing bodily injury must be reported to the police, and if you fail to stop to give assistance you may face a jail sentence. Jail is also a possible consequence of drink-driving, about which the police are very strict. Illegal parking will also be treated severely, your number-plates being removed and only returned after payment of a 5,000-drachma fine. Hire cars and foreign drivers are not exempted.
See also **Car Rental** (page 111).

Electricity
Voltage is 220 AC, and most normal electrical gadgets such as hairdryers will work, although visitors from some countries will need a converter while others will require an adaptor for the European round two-pin sockets used in Athens.

Embassies
Australia
D Soutsou 37 (tel: 644-7303)
Canada
Gennadiou 1 (tel: 723-9511)
Ireland
Vasileos Konstandinou 7 (tel: 723-2771)
New Zealand
An. Tsoha 15–17 (tel: 641-0311/5)
United Kingdom
Ploutarchou 1 (tel: 723-6211)
USA
Vasilissis Sofias 91 (tel: 721-2951)

Emergency Telephone Numbers
For a medical emergency in Athens call 166, or 171 for the Tourist Police who can also help with medical matters.

Health
No certificates of inoculation or vaccination are required by citizens of the EU, US, Canada, Australia and New Zealand, but it is a good idea to have a typhoid-cholera booster and ensure that you have had recent tetanus and polio jabs. Tap water is safe to drink. Greek pharmacists are highly trained and often multilingual, and for minor ailments can offer advice and a prescription. Look for the green cross sign or ask for the *farmakio*. State hospitals offer free emergency medical attention to EU citizens holding form E111 (although 'free' can mean paying on the spot and claiming a refund when you get home). Should you need lengthier attention, you would

be advised to seek private treatment, which is superior to basic state care. Insurance is obviously essential. Most doctors, like pharmacists, are well trained and usually speak English. The telephone number of the State Hospital for Athens is 777-8901. Dial 105 for details of doctors on call.

Athens in summer can be a cauldron, with an increasing number of heatwaves in recent years taking the midsummer temperatures soaring above 40°C. Combined with the smog, which various governments have tried in vain to do something about, this has on occasion caused high numbers of fatalities among elderly Athenians and cannot be ignored. Try to avoid August, and try to do your sightseeing

A shop for the olive connoisseur, with an embarrassment of choice

early or late in the day. Even in spring and autumn, when the sun may be pleasant rather than fierce, do not forget to cover up if out for some time.

Holidays

Public holidays are 1 January, 25 March, Good Friday until noon, Easter Sunday, 1 May, 25 and 26 December; museums and sites are closed on these days. In addition there are half-holidays, when weekend opening hours apply, these being 6 January, the first Monday of Orthodox Lent (called *Kathara Dheftera* – Clean Monday), Easter Saturday, Easter Monday, Whit Sunday, 15 August and 28 October.

Lost Property

If you lose something there is a strong chance it will still be there if you return to where you left it, as most Greeks are very

honest. If you don't know where it went missing, report the loss to the hotel management or call Lost and Found on 770-5771 (or 523-0111 if you lose something in a bus or taxi).

Media
Television
Greece's two state-owned television channels, ERT 1 and ERT 2, both broadcast a number of American TV programmes and international films with Greek subtitles. An increasing number of satellite channels can be received.

Radio
The two state channels are also called ERT 1 and ERT 2, though ERT1 is divided up into three programmes on different

City-centre news-stand

frequencies. On the First Programme a multilingual news programme is broadcast covering English, French, German and Arabic at 07.40hrs each morning (728KHz). English-only news bulletins are also broadcast daily at 14.00 and 21.00hrs on ERT 2 (98KHz). Try 9.41, 12.09 or 15.07MHz for the BBC World Service with news on the hour, and 1484 and 1594KHz for the American Forces Radio Service, also with news on the hour.

Magazines and Newspapers
Most major European newspapers are widely available on the evening of the day of publication, or the

following morning. American newspapers and international magazines are also available, but expensive. Try the kiosks on Syntagma, or around the Plaka district. **Reymond's** at Voukourestiou 18 (tel: 364-8187) stocks many foreign-language books, magazines and newspapers.

There are several English-language publications which carry information on local events and temporary exhibitions. Look for the daily (except Monday) *Athens News*, the *Greek Weekly News*, the excellent weekly guide *Athenscope* and two monthlies – *Athenian* and *30 Days: Greece This Month*. All are easily found in shops and at kiosks.

Money Matters

The Greek currency is the drachma. There are still 1- and 2-drachma coins, but these are of such low value that change is normally given to the nearest 5 drachma, increasingly the nearest 10. Other coins are for 20, 50 and 100 drachma; notes are in denominations of 50, 100, 500, 1,000 and 5,000 drachma. Visitors may import up to 100,000 drachma into the country and take 20,000 out. Have some small denomination notes on arrival. Travellers' cheques to any amount can be imported and exported, but foreign currency of more than the equivalent of 1,000 US dollars should be declared at customs. Travellers' cheques can be changed at most banks, hotels and post offices, on production of a passport. Some shops and restaurants will also change them – at a less favourable rate

of exchange. Post offices generally charge a lower commission than banks or tourist exchanges. Look for the yellow English-language 'EXCHANGE' sign. Banks and post offices are generally open from 08.00 or 08.30 to14.00hrs, weekdays only (13.30 hrs Fridays).

You still cannot easily travel in Greece with just 'plastic' money. It is normal to settle even large transactions in cash, and 'No cheques' is a common sign, even in Athens hotels. However, Eurocheques are widely accepted in banks (but not necessarily elsewhere), while credit cards are increasingly accepted in the more expensive hotels, shops and restaurants.

Opening Times
Banks
See **Money Matters**, above.

Museums and Sites
Official opening hours change from year to year, and from winter to summer. The actual opening hours may also frequently be different from the official ones. This book gives current summer opening hours (1 April to 31 October) unless otherwise stated, but always check first if planning to set out on a special trip.

Shops
In summer shops generally open from 08.00 through to 13.00hrs, when they close for the afternoon siesta. Evening opening is from about 17.00 to 20.00hrs, although some supermarkets and tourist shops stay open

DIRECTORY

much later. Opening and closing times may vary by an hour or so, but all will close during the afternoon. Shops are generally closed on Sundays, except for tourist shops and some other shops in central Athens. These times will vary in winter.

Pharmacies

Ask for the *farmakío* or look for the sign of the green cross. Greek pharmacists have medical training and can advise on common ailments. If you need prescription drugs, remember to take the exact details with you in case you need extra supplies. Note that the common painkiller codeine is banned in Greece and you can be fined for carrying it. Pharmacies open the usual shop hours, but close on Saturdays and Sundays. A 24-hour rota system operates outside normal hours, and each shop will display a notice with details (in Greek) of the nearest open pharmacy. Dial 107 for details of 24-hour pharmacies.

Places of Worship

The majority of Greeks belong to the Greek Orthodox church and Athens has as many Orthodox churches as you would expect. Many are always open, but those with precious icons or other valuables may be locked. Sunday services start early in the morning (about 07.30 or 08.00hrs) and go on for hours. Many worshippers attend only part of the service. Visitors are accepted, but should dress decently and behave discreetly. In Athens other denominations include the Roman Catholic

Church of Ayios Dhionysios on Omirou, the Anglican Church of Ayios Pavlos at Filellinon 29 and the nearby Russian Orthodox Church of Ayios Nikodemos. There are also two Protestant churches: the German Evangelical Christos Kirche at Sina 66 and the American inter-denominational church of St Andrew at Papanikole 3, Papagou.

Police

The affairs of visitors are the responsibility of the Tourist Police, a separate branch of the police force whose officers are usually fluent in at least one foreign language. They make regular checks on facilities and prices in hotels and restaurants, and should be your first call (tel: 171) if you find yourself in trouble – from a dispute with a taxi driver to the unlikely event of a serious crime. Often an insistence that the problem be resolved by the Tourist Police is enough for the other side to back down, if they are in the wrong. The Tourist Police have the power not only to fine people but to remove their licences to operate, so this could be a serious matter for anyone trying to trick a visitor. Such disputes are, however, rare. See also **Emergency Telephone Numbers,** page 114.

Post Offices

To find one, look out for the yellow ELTA sign. Many post offices cash travellers' cheques and exchange currency: look for the 'EXCHANGE' sign. They are normally open morning shop hours only, except for the central post office at Eolou 100

Greek Orthodox priest in church.
Visitors are welcome at services

(near Omonia), which is open Monday to Saturday, 07.30–20.30hrs, and the large post office at the junction of Syntagma and Mitropoleos, which is additionally open on Sunday from 07.30 to13.30hrs. Queues can be long and slow, as post office counters offer a range of services. If you only want stamps (*grammatosima*) for a postcard, or for a letter up to 20gms, try kiosks or shops selling postcards as they frequently also stock these small denomination stamps. If you need to post a parcel, this must be inspected by the post office clerk before sealing. This is why you will see people in queues carrying wrapping paper and string.

Post boxes are small yellow boxes, with no distinguishing features unless you find one with two slots, in which case *Exoteriko* is for overseas mail. Air-mail letters take three to six days to reach the rest of Europe, five to eight days for North America, slightly longer for Australasia. Postcards take longer.

Public Transport

Buses and Trolleys

Buses are cheap and reasonably regular, but invariably crowded. Smoking is banned for passengers. Greek National Tourist Organisation (GNTO or EOT) offices can provide timetables of services from Athens, and a route map

DIRECTORY

for city services is available from the tourist office in Athens (see **Tourist Offices**, page 123). Both buses and trolleys display their number and destination at the front. Before boarding, you must buy a flat-fare ticket at the ticket booths near most stops or from news kiosks. On boarding the bus, stamp your own ticket in the machines just inside the doors. The main bus station for services to places such as Marathón, Soúnion and Vravróna is on Mavromateon, at the northwest corner of the National Archaeological Museum. The buses are orange, with blue buses and yellow trolleys serving Athens and the immediate suburbs. Services to the Peloponnese and northwest Greece leave from Terminal A, which is at Kifissou 100, and to most other places from Terminal B, at Liossion 260.

Save your legs by taking the funicular to the top of Likavitós

Ferries
See under **Arriving** (page 110) for boat services to Piraeus, the port of Athens. Be aware that there are several different harbours in Piraeus, quite some distance apart, and it is important to establish which one your boat will be leaving from. Obtain an up-to-date timetable from the Greek National Tourist Organisation (though there may be late changes).

Trains
The state-owned rail network (OSE) is limited and rail travel, though even cheaper than bus, is usually slower. There are two main stations, next to each other on Deligianni. Peloponissou serves Kórinthos and the Peloponnese, and Larissis the rest of Greece. Timetables can be obtained from GNTO offices, but as with ferries these are often subject to late changes.

Metro
The city's one metro line runs from the northern suburb of Kifisiá, where there are campsites and hotels, through central Athens and out to the port of Piraeus to the south. Convenient central stops include Omonia Square and Monastiráki for the Plaka and the Acropolis. The service runs every 4 to 10 minutes, from 05.30 to midnight. There are three zones: A from Piraeus to Monastiráki, B from Omonia to Patissia and C from Perissos to Kifisiá. There is a flat fare per journey per zone, and tickets can be bought at any station from manned kiosks or automatic machines which

accept coins up to 50 drachma. Stamp your ticket as you pass through the entrance gates. Not all trains run the full length of the line, so check the destination board.

Taxis

Taxis are cheap by comparison with other countries, and it is quite usual to use them for much longer journeys than you might contemplate elsewhere. Most are metered, but see under **Arriving** (page 109) for possible problems. Drivers are allowed to stop to pick up other passengers going in the same direction, each paying their share of the fare when they leave (the interpretation of 'same direction' is up to the driver). Because Greeks use taxis constantly, and half the private cars are banned from central Athens on any one day (see **Driving**, page 113), it can be hard to find an available taxi: book ahead if the journey is important.

Senior Citizens

The midsummer Athenian heat is fierce, and a sudden heatwave – with the attendant increase in pollution – can be lethal, particularly to the elderly. Consider travelling before July or after mid-September, when the weather will be hot but not deadly.
If you like to sit and watch the world go by, you already have a great deal in common with the senior citizens of Greece ... and the ideal place in which to do it. For those who like to get out and about but do not wish to drive, there are numerous coach trips taking in the classical sites, picking passengers up at the larger central Athens hotels. If you cannot afford to stay in such a hotel, try to make your base near Syntagma or, if you're unlikely to want to venture outside Athens, near the Plaka district.

Student and Youth Travel

There are both official and private Youth Hostels in Athens (see **Accommodation** on page 95 for some details). They are cheap and basic, and you need an International Youth Hostel Card. These can be bought on arrival or in advance from the **Greek Association of Youth Hostels**, Dragatsaniou 4, Athens (tel: 323-4107). There is also a YWCA but no YMCA. An International Student Identity Card can provide travel discounts and cheap entry to museums and classical sites.

Telephones

The easiest way to make a call is to use a metered public telephone. Many street-corner kiosks and ordinary shops have these phones; they are so commonplace that they do not usually warrant a special sign. You simply dial the number you require and the meter will show the amount to pay at the end of the call. This saves having to amass piles of 10, 20 and 50 drachma coins to call abroad, these being the only coins accepted by pay-phones (an orange stripe indicates an international phone). Direct-dial phones are fairly common in good hotels, but charges are much higher than for metered phones.

DIRECTORY

There are also metered phones in some branches of the OTE (Greek Telecommunications Organisation). These are sometimes in the main post office, sometimes in a separate building, and again you pay at the end of the call. These phones may be available at times other than normal opening hours.

Cheap rates for calls within Greece apply 15.00–17.00hrs, 21.00–08.00hrs and at weekends. For international calls from Athens, there is a small discount between 22.00 and 08.00hrs. Connections for international calls are surprisingly good, though it is important to dial slowly. Dialling codes from within Greece are:

```
Australia..........................006
Canada and
the USA ...........................001
Eire ..............................00353
New Zealand................0064
UK..................................0044
International Operator ..161
```

You should then omit the first zero of your local area code. In this guide, the 01 local area code for all Athens numbers has been omitted from entries. If calling to Greece from abroad, use your own international code for Greece then the Greek number, omitting the first zero of the local area code.

Time

Athens is two hours ahead of Greenwich Mean Time in winter, one hour ahead of the rest of western Europe, seven hours ahead of US and Canada Eastern Standard Time, ten hours for Pacific Standard Time, and eight hours behind Australian New South Wales time. Greek Summer Time begins and ends simultaneously with the rest of Europe (except UK), but this may not coincide with time changes in other countries, such as the USA. Take care if travelling at those times, especially in spring when an hour is lost and ferries and flights could be missed. Dial 141 for a recorded time message in Greek.

Tipping

Service (15 per cent) is included in restaurants but it is normal to leave on the table any small change after paying the bill (100 drachma notes could be regarded as small change). If you are particularly pleased with the service, a tip of a few hundred drachma would not be over-generous. A small note is also appreciated by the wine waiter or the boy who clears the table.

In hotels you will seldom feel obliged to tip, but a small gratuity to the porter or barman of a 100 drachma note will be welcomed. For chambermaids, 100 drachma per day left at the end of the stay would be generous. For taxi drivers, 'keep the change' is the usual practice.

Toilets

Public toilets in Athens are few and far between and best avoided. Finding a friendly taverna is the best option, but standards still vary enormously. Greek plumbing pipes have probably not improved in the

There is no difficulty in finding a ferry agent in Piraeus

last 2,000 years: they are of a small non-standard bore, and easily become blocked if toilet paper is flushed down them. It is only the most modern hotels that have more up-to-date plumbing, and even in these you may need to check first. In bathrooms and toilets elsewhere you will find a waste bin for the disposal of toilet paper, tampons and sanitary towels. It may seem unhygienic, but you will become accustomed to the practice and it is better than a blocked pipe flooding the room when you try to flush the toilet.

Tourist Offices

The Greek National Tourist Organisation (GNTO or, in Greece, EOT) has offices in:

Australia
51–7 Pitt Street, Sydney, NSW 2000 (tel: 02-241-1663)

Canada
1300 Bay Street, Main Level, Toronto, Ontario M5R 3K8 (tel: 416-968-2220)
1223 Rue de la Montagne, Montreal, Quebec H3G 1Z2 (tel: 514-871-1535)

United Kingdom
4 Conduit Street, London W1R 0DJ (tel: 0171-734-5997)

United States of America
645 Fifth Avenue, New York, NY 10022 (tel: 212-421-5777)
168 North Michigan Avenue, Chicago IL 60601 (tel: 312-782-1084)
611 West 6th St, Suite 2998, Los Angeles, CA 90017 (tel: 213-626-6696)
The principal office for Athens is in Syntagma Square, inside the National Bank of Greece building (tel: 322-2545). Opening hours are Monday to Friday, 08.00–20.00 hrs, Saturday 08.00–14.00 hrs. The Head Office for written enquiries is at Amerikis 2, PO Box 1017 (tel: 322-3111).

LANGUAGE

Unless you know the Greek
script, a vocabulary will not be
of very much use. But it is
helpful to know the alphabet, so
that you can find your way
around; and the following few
transliterated basic words and
phrases will help too. (See also
Food and Drink pages 82–4).

Alphabet

Alpha	Aα	short a, as in hat
Beta	Bβ	v sound
Gamma	Γγ	guttural g sound
Delta	Δδ	hard th, as in father
Epsilon	Eε	short e
Zita	Zζ	z sound
Eta	Hη	long e, as in feet
Theta	Θθ	soft th, as in think
Iota	Iι	short i, as in hit
Kappa	Kκ	k sound
Lambda	Λλ	l sound
Mu	Mμ	m sound
Nu	Nν	n sound
Xi	Ξξ	x or ks sound
Omicron	Oo	short o, as in pot
Pi	Ππ	p sound
Rho	Pρ	r sound
Sigma	Σσ	s sound
Taf	Ττ	t sound
Ipsilon	Yυ	another ee sound, or y as in funny
Phi	Φφ	f sound
Chi	Χχ	guttural ch, as in loch
Psi	Ψψ	ps, as in chops
Omega	Ωω	long o, as in bone

Numbers

1	éna
2	dío
3	tria
4	téssera
5	pénde
6	éxi
7	eptá
8	októ
9	ennía
10	déka
11	éndeka
12	dódeka
13	dekatría
14	dekatéssera
15	dekapénde
16	dekaéxi
17	dekaeptá
18	dekaokto
19	dekaennía
20	ikosi
30	triánda
40	saránda
50	peninda
100	ekató
101	ekaton éna
1000	chília

Basic vocabulary

good morning	kaliméra
good evening	kalispéra
goodnight	kaliníkta
goodbye	chérete
hello	yásou
thank you	efharistó
please/you're welcome	parakaló
yes	ne
no	óchi
where is...?	poo íne?
how much is..?	póso káni?
I would like	tha íthela
do you speak English?	milate angliká?
I don't speak Greek	then miló elliniká
I beg your pardon (apology)	signómi

Places
street	ódos
square	platía
restaurant	estiatório
hotel	xenodochío
room	domátio
post office	tachithromío
police	astinomía
pharmacy	farmakío
doctor	iatrós
bank	trápeza
hospital	nosokomío
café	kafeneion

Travelling
car	aftokínito
bus	leoforío
train	tréno
boat	karávi
garage	garáz
airport	aerodrómio
ticket	isitírio

Food and drink
food	fagitó
bread	psomí
water	neró
wine	krasí
beer	bira
coffee	kafé

Fish
lobster	astakós
squid	kalamarákia
octopus	oktapóthi
red mullet	barboúnia
whitebait	marídes

Meat/poultry
lamb	arnáki
chicken	kotópoulo
meat balls	kefthédes
meat on a skewer	
	souvlákia

Vegetables
spinach	spanáki
courgette	kolokithia
beans	fasólia

Salads and starters
olives	eliés
yoghurt and cucumber dip	
	tzatsiki
tomato and cucumber salad	
	angour domata
stuffed vine leaves	
	dolmades
'Greek' salad with cheese	
	horiatiki

A Note on Transliteration

The Greek alphabet cannot be transliterated into other languages in a straightforward manner. This means that romanised spellings of Greek words can vary. In place-name headings, and in the Index, this book uses the transliterations that correspond to AA maps. More familiar anglicised spellings (given in brackets in the headings) are sometimes used in the text. This inevitably leads to inconsistencies when compared to other books, leaflets and road signs However, the differences are seldom so great as to make a name unrecognisable. Similarly there may be differing translations of the names of museums and other places of interest, so that what one source interprets as 'Historical and Ethnological Museum' may elsewhere be termed 'National Historical Museum'. To avoid confusion, headings give the name in romanised Greek, followed by the most usual English translation in brackets.

INDEX

INDEX

Acknowledgements

The Automobile Association wishes to thank the following photographers and libraries for their assistance in the preparation of this book.

BRITISH MUSEUM 34/5.

J. ALLAN CASH PHOTOLIBRARY 57.

MARY EVANS PICTURE LIBRARY 10, 12, 14.

NATIONAL GALLERY OF ATHENS 30.

NATURE PHOTOGRAPHERS LTD 76 (A. J. Cleeve), 77 (R. Tidman).

The remaining photographs are held in the Automobile Association's own library (© AA PHOTO LIBRARY) and were taken by **Peter Wilson** for this book.

Contributors
Copy editor: Audrey Horne   **Verifier**: Colin Follett
Indexer: Marie Lorimer